ANIMALS

How to Use Your SD-X Reader with This Book

This highly informative book introduces you and your child to animals in a new interactive format. You can read the book and study the rich illustrations, but a touch of the SD-X Reader adds in-depth audio information, word definitions, and learning games to the pictures and text.

1. Press the Power button to turn the SD-X Reader on or off. The LED will light up when the SD-X Reader is on.

2. Touch the volume buttons found on this page or on the Table of Contents page in this book to adjust the volume.

3. Throughout the book, words in this color provide additional information when they're touched with the SD-X Reader. Objects on the page may play additional audio.

4. At the top left corner of each spread, you'll see circles like these: ⬤ ⬤ Touch a circle to start a learning game or quiz. Touch the same circle again to stop playing the game. Touch another circle to start another learning game or quiz.

5. Some learning games will ask you to use Ⓣ Ⓕ buttons or Ⓐ Ⓑ buttons to answer. For other learning games, touch objects on the page to answer.

6. When you've answered all the questions in a learning game, you'll hear your score.

7. After two minutes of inactivity, the SD-X Reader will beep and go to sleep.

8. If the batteries are low, the SD-X Reader will beep twice and the LED will start blinking. Replace the batteries by following the instructions on the next page. The SD-X Reader uses two AAA batteries.

9. To use headphones or earbuds, plug them into the headphone jack on the bottom of the SD-X Reader.

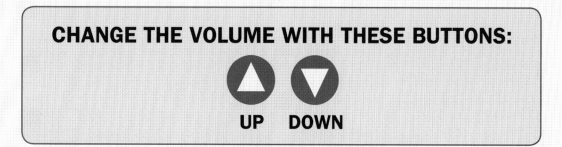

CHANGE THE VOLUME WITH THESE BUTTONS:

🔼 🔽

UP   DOWN

Battery Information

Includes two replaceable AAA batteries (UM-4 or LR03).

Battery Installation

1. Open battery door with small screwdriver.
2. Install new batteries according to +/- polarity. If batteries are not installed properly, the device will not function.
3. Replace battery door; secure with small screw.

Battery Safety

Batteries must be replaced by adults only. Properly dispose of used batteries. See battery manufacturer for disposal recommendations. Do not mix alkaline, standard (carbon-zinc), or rechargeable (nickel-cadmium) batteries. Do not mix old and new batteries. Only recommended batteries of the same or equivalent type should be used. Remove weakened or dead batteries. Never short-circuit the supply terminals. Non-rechargeable batteries are not to be recharged. Do not use rechargeable batteries. If batteries are swallowed, in the USA, promptly see a doctor and have the doctor phone 1-202-625-3333 collect. In other countries, have the doctor call your local poison control center. This product uses 2 AAA batteries (2 X 1.5V = 3.0 V). Use batteries of the same or equivalent type as recommended. The supply terminals are not to be short-circuited. Batteries should be changed when sounds mix, distort, or become otherwise unintelligible as batteries weaken. The electrostatic discharge may interfere with the sound module. If this occurs, please simply restart the sound module by pressing any key.

In Europe, the dustbin symbol indicates that batteries, rechargeable batteries, button cells, battery packs, and similar materials must not be discarded in household waste. Batteries containing hazardous substances are harmful to the environment and to health. Please help to protect the environment from health risks by telling your children to dispose of batteries properly and by taking batteries to local collection points. Batteries handled in this manner are safely recycled.

Warning: Changes or modifications to this unit not expressly approved by the party responsible for compliance could void the user's authority to operate the equipment.

NOTE: This equipment has been tested and found to comply with the limits for a Class B digital device, pursuant to Part 15 of the FCC Rules. These limits are designed to provide reasonable protection against harmful interference in a residential installation. This equipment generates, uses, and can radiate radio frequency energy and, if not installed and used in accordance with the instructions, may cause harmful interference to radio communications. However, there is no guarantee that interference will not occur in a particular installation. If this equipment does cause harmful interference to radio or television reception, which can be determined by turning the equipment off and on, the user is encouraged to try to correct the interference by one or more of the following measures: Reorient or relocate the receiving antenna. Increase the separation between the equipment and receiver. Connect the equipment into an outlet on a circuit different from that to which the receiver is connected. Consult the dealer or an experienced radio TV technician for help.

Published by Louis Weber, C.E.O., Publications International, Ltd.
8140 Lehigh Avenue
Morton Grove, Illinois 60053

Customer Service: Customer_Service@pubint.com

www.pilbooks.com

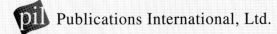 Publications International, Ltd.

Manufactured in China.

8 7 6 5 4 3 2 1

ISBN: 978-1-60553-906-5

CONTENTS

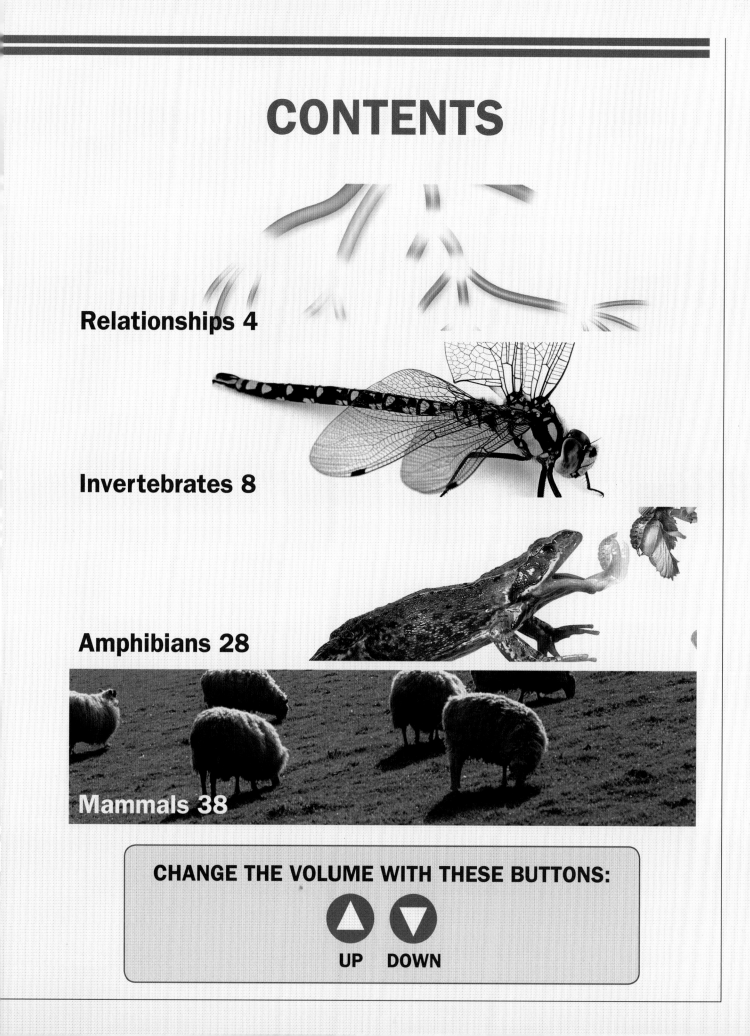

CHANGE THE VOLUME WITH THESE BUTTONS:

▲ ▼

UP DOWN

The Tree of Life

Here is a visual representation to explain how all living beings are related. *Phylogenetic* trees use information from fossils as well as that generated through the structural and molecular studies of organisms. The construction of phylogenetic trees takes into account the theory of *evolution*, which indicates that organisms are descendants of a common ancestor.

Eukaryota

This group consists of species that have a true nucleus in their cellular structure.

Animals

Multicellular organisms

CNIDARIANS

BILATERAL

Archaea

Unicellular and microscopic organisms

Plants

Multicellular organisms

NOT VASCULAR

VASCULAR

VERTEBRATES

EURYARCHAEOTA

KORARCHAEOTA

WITH SEED

MOLLUSKS

TETRAPODS

CRENARCHAEOTA

SEEDLESS

CARTILAGINOUS FISH

ANGIOSPERM

AMPHIBIANS

Relationships

The scientific evidence supports the theory that life on Earth has evolved and that all species share common ancestors. However, there are no conclusive facts about the origin of life.

GYMNOSPERM

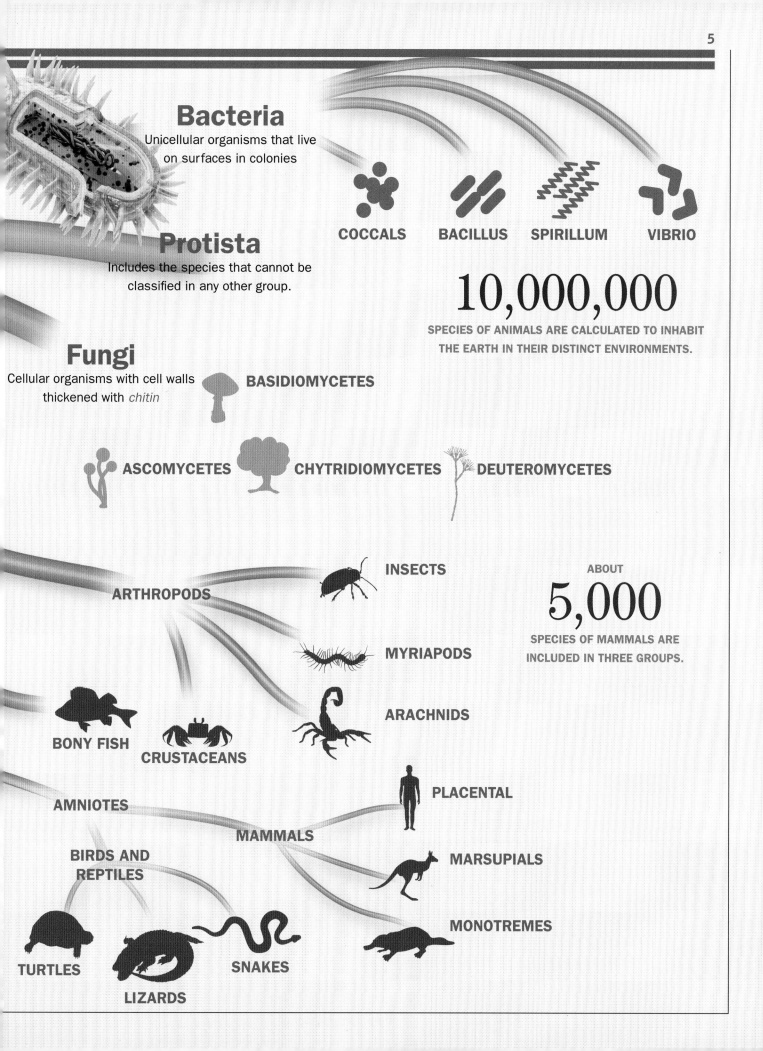

Bacteria
Unicellular organisms that live on surfaces in colonies

COCCALS **BACILLUS** **SPIRILLUM** **VIBRIO**

Protista
Includes the species that cannot be classified in any other group.

10,000,000
SPECIES OF ANIMALS ARE CALCULATED TO INHABIT THE EARTH IN THEIR DISTINCT ENVIRONMENTS.

Fungi
Cellular organisms with cell walls thickened with *chitin*

BASIDIOMYCETES

ASCOMYCETES **CHYTRIDIOMYCETES** **DEUTEROMYCETES**

INSECTS

ABOUT
5,000
SPECIES OF MAMMALS ARE INCLUDED IN THREE GROUPS.

ARTHROPODS

MYRIAPODS

ARACHNIDS

BONY FISH

CRUSTACEANS

PLACENTAL

AMNIOTES

MAMMALS

MARSUPIALS

BIRDS AND REPTILES

MONOTREMES

TURTLES **SNAKES**

LIZARDS

Through Time

Geologic structures and *fossils* have been used by scientists to reconstruct the history of life on our planet. Scientists believe that the Earth was formed about 4.6 billion years ago and that the first living beings, single-celled organisms, appeared about one billion years later. The study of fossils can provide an account of plants and animals that have disappeared from the Earth.

PRECAMBRIAN TIME BROUGHT...

THE FORMATION OF THE CRUST

LAVA BECAME ROCK.

THE PRESENCE OF OXYGEN

THE FIRST EVIDENCE OF LIFE

Fossils that date back some 3.5 billion years show the first evidence of life on the planet.

MULTICELLULAR ANIMALS

4.6 BILLION YEARS AGO

1 BILLION YEARS AGO

THE PALEOZOIC ERA BROUGHT...

THE CAMBRIAN EXPLOSION

Numerous multicellular species suddenly appeared.

A SPONGELIKE ANIMAL

A MARINE INVERTEBRATE

THE CONQUEST OF EARTH

AN EARLY FISH

AN ANCIENT AMPHIBIAN

ANCIENT FISH SCALES

270 MILLION YEARS AGO

MASSIVE EXTINCTIONS

MASS EXTINCTIONS		60% OF SPECIES ●	80% OF SPECIES ●		95% OF SPECIES ●	
4.6-2.5 BILLION YEARS AGO	2.5 BILLION-542 MILLION YEARS AGO	542 - 488	488 - 444	444 - 416	416 - 359	359 - 299	299 - 251
ARCHEAN EON	PROTEROZOIC EON	CAMBRIAN	ORDOVICIAN	SILURIAN	DEVONIAN	CARBONIF-EROUS	PERMIAN
PRECAMBRIAN TIME		**PALEOZOIC ERA**					

The Timeline

4.8 billion years ago
Formation of the Earth

3 billion years ago
The first bacteria appear.

2.1 billion years ago
Oxygen appears in the atmosphere.

600 million years ago
First fossils of multicellular animals

PRECAMBRIAN

PALEOZOIC

MESOZOIC

CENOZOIC

THE MESOZOIC ERA BROUGHT...

THE ERA OF REPTILES

A CHANGING WORLD

NEW TYPES OF ANIMALS

PREDATORS

THE HEAVYWEIGHT BAROSAURUS

A BAROSAURUS VERTEBRA

200 MILLION YEARS AGO

THE CENOZOIC ERA BROUGHT...

A CHANGING CLIMATE

THE DEVELOPMENT OF BIRDS AND MAMMALS

FEATHERED

SABER TEETH

EARLY HUMAN RELATIVES

50 MILLION YEARS AGO

75% OF SPECIES

251 - 200	200 - 146	146 - 65.5	65.5 - 23	SINCE 23 MILLION YEARS AGO
TRIASSIC	JURASSIC	CRETACEOUS	PALEOGENE	NEOGENE
MESOZOIC ERA			**CENOZOIC ERA**	

The First Conquest

To be able to live on land, *invertebrates* developed ways of breathing and moving that were adapted to a land environment. Thus insects, which can walk and fly, have populated land and air environments.

MONARCH BUTTERFLY

ASIAN TIGER MOSQUITO

CRAMER'S BLUE MORPHO

PRAYING MANTIS

70%
OF THE SPECIES THAT LIVE IN TREES ARE INSECTS.

The Order of the Food Chain

Spiders

Ladybugs

Fleas

FIRST LEVEL	SECOND LEVEL	THIRD LEVEL

The Most Successful

Beetles are the most prolific and diverse group of the animal kingdom.

OVER

350,000

SPECIES OF BEETLES ARE KNOWN

COMMON FURNITURE BEETLE

Tunnels bored by beetles

FEEDING ON DEAD MATTER

TICK

BROWN GARDEN SNAIL

BURYING BEETLE

BLACK VINE WEEVIL

SILVERFISH

Small Arthropods

Most land- and air-dwelling arthropods have air tubes that supply oxygen directly to the cells and tissues.

CLICK BEETLE

PILLBUGS

CENTIPEDE

DESERT MILLIPEDE

EUROPEAN HORNET

WASP

Naturally Programmed

The world of air- and land-dwelling invertebrates includes societies, such as those of bees, wasps, and ants.

BLOOD-RED ANT (WORKER)

SPIDER

SILKWORM

EARTHWORM

A Special Family

The *arachnid* family includes spiders, scorpions, fleas, ticks, and mites. Arachnids were the first *arthropods* to live on land. The fossil remains of scorpions are found beginning in the Silurian Period, and they show that these animals have not undergone major changes.

GIANT HOUSEHOLD SPIDER

The female can transport up to 30 offspring on its back.

PEDIPALPS

EMPEROR SCORPION

The claws hold the prey and immobilize it.

CHELICERAE move up and down. In the more primitive spiders, the chelicerae move side to side.

Mites and Ticks

Saliva glands

Tick

Middle stomach

Palps

Adhesion material

Infection

TICK

MITE

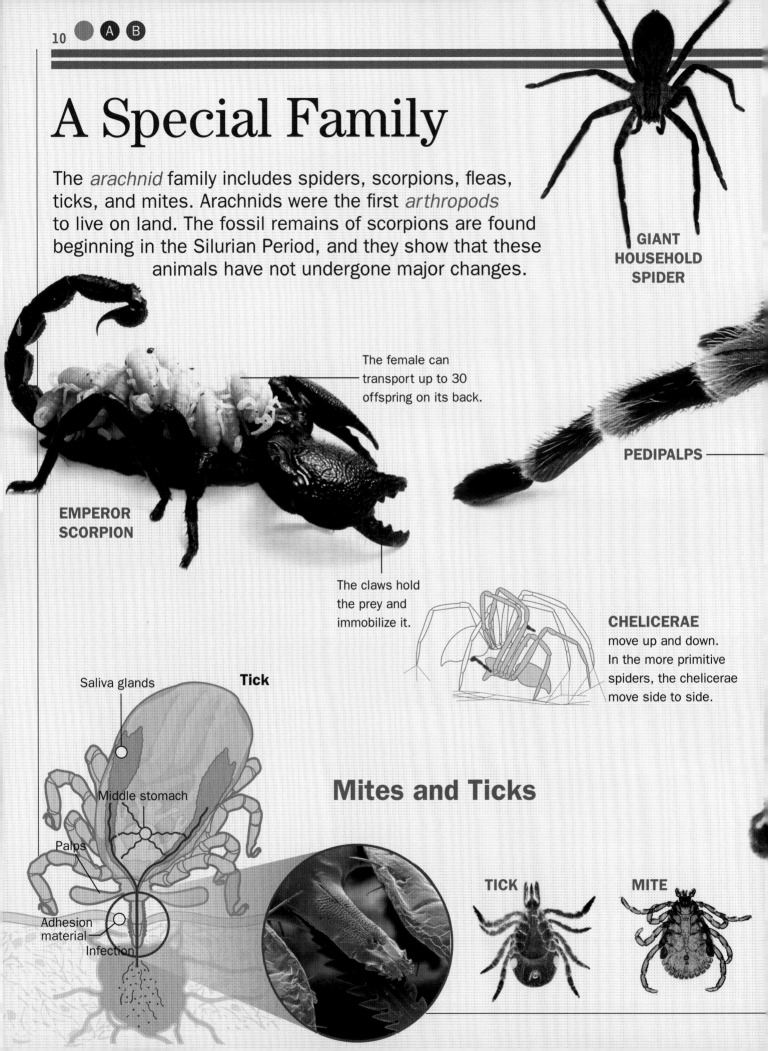

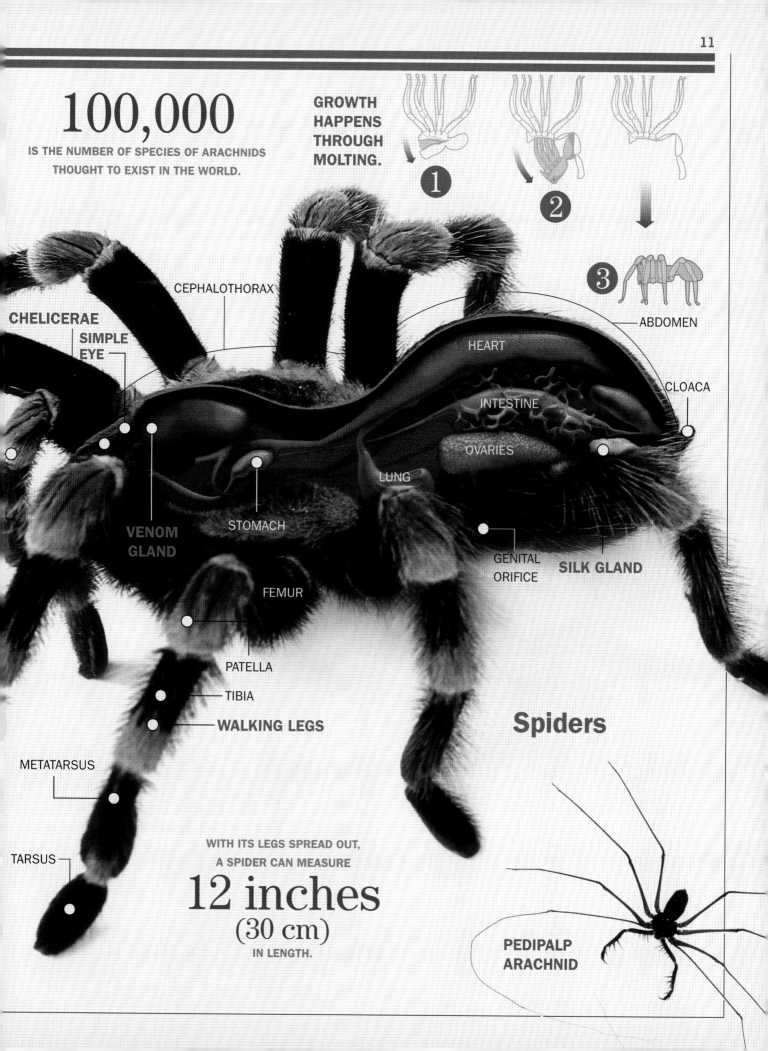

100,000

IS THE NUMBER OF SPECIES OF ARACHNIDS
THOUGHT TO EXIST IN THE WORLD.

**GROWTH
HAPPENS
THROUGH
MOLTING.**

1

2

3

CEPHALOTHORAX

CHELICERAE

SIMPLE
EYE

ABDOMEN

HEART

CLOACA

INTESTINE

OVARIES

LUNG

VENOM
GLAND

STOMACH

GENITAL
ORIFICE   **SILK GLAND**

FEMUR

PATELLA

TIBIA

WALKING LEGS

Spiders

METATARSUS

TARSUS

WITH ITS LEGS SPREAD OUT,
A SPIDER CAN MEASURE

12 inches
(30 cm)
IN LENGTH.

**PEDIPALP
ARACHNID**

Poisonous Sting

Venomous arachnids are the group of *arthropods* most feared by people. Even if a bite may be fatal to another animal, it is unlikely that it will be fatal to a human being, who would be attacked only as a means of defense in cases of fear or danger. The scorpion stands out among the most dangerous species. It uses its stinger when it wants to be certain of catching a difficult prey. Another notable example is the black widow, whose tiny body produces one third as much *venom* as a rattlesnake.

Out of 38,000 known
spider species

30
species

have truly dangerous venom.

1 DETECTS THE PREY

PALP OR PEDIPALP

CHELICERAE

HUNTING SPIDER

VENOM CONTAINS MANY SUBSTANCES

2 CLOSES IN

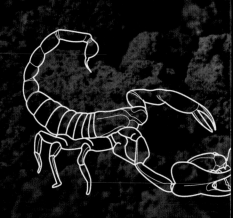

TELSON
STINGER

TAIL

VENOM GLANDS

MUSCLES

The only places in the world where there are no scorpions are

Antarctica
and
Greenland.

ABDOMEN

Scorpions Capture and Sting.

DESERT SCORPION

CEPHALOTHORAX

CENTRAL EYE

PECTEN

PEDIPALP

❸ ATTACK

CLAW

❹ USE OF THE STINGER

The Secret of Success

Insects and myriapods have several common features that help them succeed: sensory antennae, appendages on the head that can be used to chew, crush, or grab, highly developed eyes on the sides of the head, and pairs of jointed legs with functions that depend on the species.

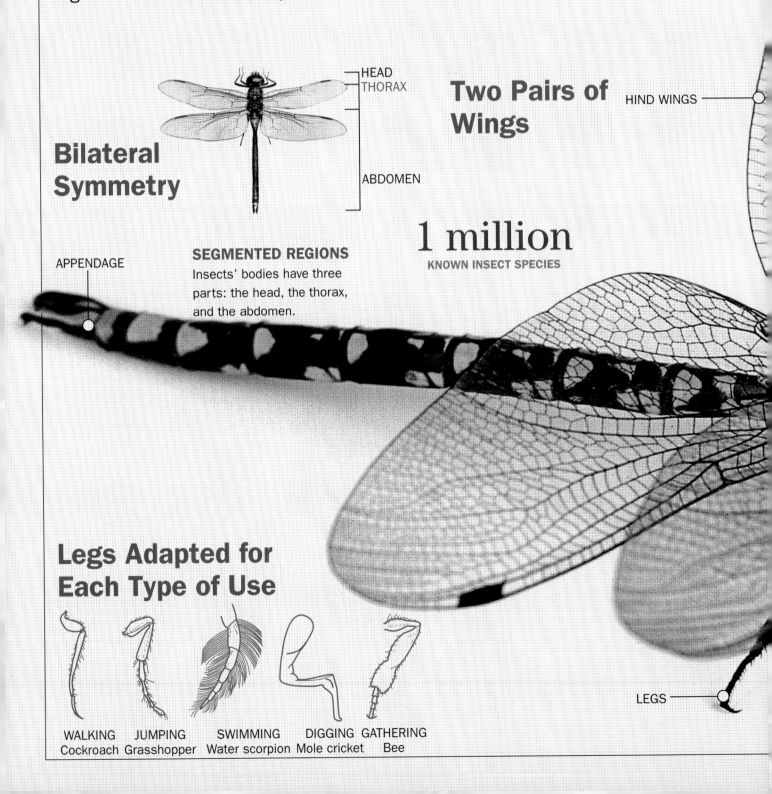

HEAD
THORAX
ABDOMEN

Two Pairs of Wings

HIND WINGS

Bilateral Symmetry

APPENDAGE

SEGMENTED REGIONS
Insects' bodies have three parts: the head, the thorax, and the abdomen.

1 million
KNOWN INSECT SPECIES

Legs Adapted for Each Type of Use

LEGS

WALKING	JUMPING	SWIMMING	DIGGING	GATHERING
Cockroach	Grasshopper	Water scorpion	Mole cricket	Bee

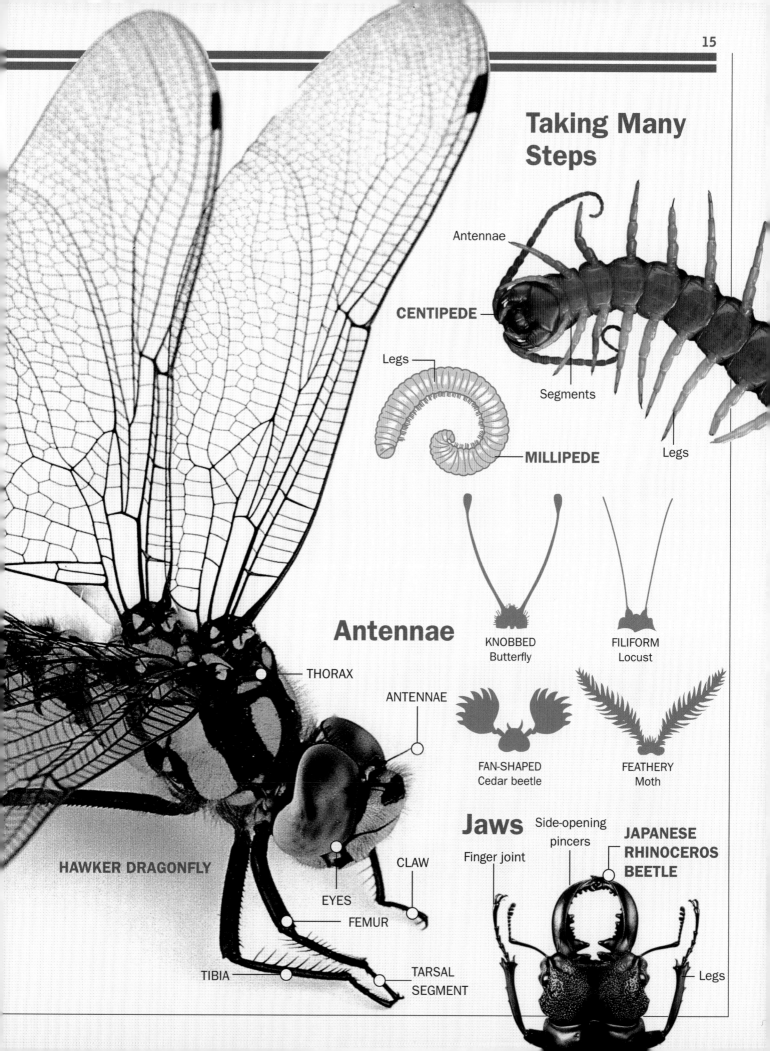

Taking Many Steps

Antennae

CENTIPEDE

Segments

Legs

Legs

MILLIPEDE

Antennae

KNOBBED
Butterfly

FILIFORM
Locust

FAN-SHAPED
Cedar beetle

FEATHERY
Moth

THORAX

ANTENNAE

HAWKER DRAGONFLY

CLAW

EYES

FEMUR

TIBIA

TARSAL
SEGMENT

Jaws

Side-opening
pincers

Finger joint

**JAPANESE
RHINOCEROS
BEETLE**

Legs

Great Walkers

Myriapod means "many feet." Centipedes and millipedes are myriapods. All are animals divided into segments. Centipedes have a pair of legs on each segment, and millipedes have two pairs of legs per segment. The legs are jointed, but they do not function independently of each other for the arthropod to move forward. The segmented body moves side to side in a regular wave pattern.

MYRIAPOD MOVEMENT

When the legs on one side of its body are closest together, those on the other side are farthest apart. This alternating pattern is repeated all along its body.

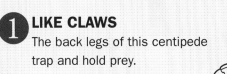

Millipedes

1 **LIKE CLAWS**
The back legs of this centipede trap and hold prey.

SIZE OR QUANTITY
Some centipedes add segments throughout their lives; others are born with a fixed number of segments that grow in size.

JOINTED FEET

VENOM GLAND

MUSCLES AND NERVES

MAXILLIPEDS

ANTENNAE

Centipedes

Scolopendrida
(MEGARIAN BANDED CENTIPEDE)

TYPICAL SIZE	4 INCHES (10 CM)
MAXIMUM SIZE	12 INCHES (30 CM)
QUANTITY OF SEGMENTS	20-40

2 DEADLY WEAPON
The venom is discharged
through the opening at
the tip of the maxillipeds.

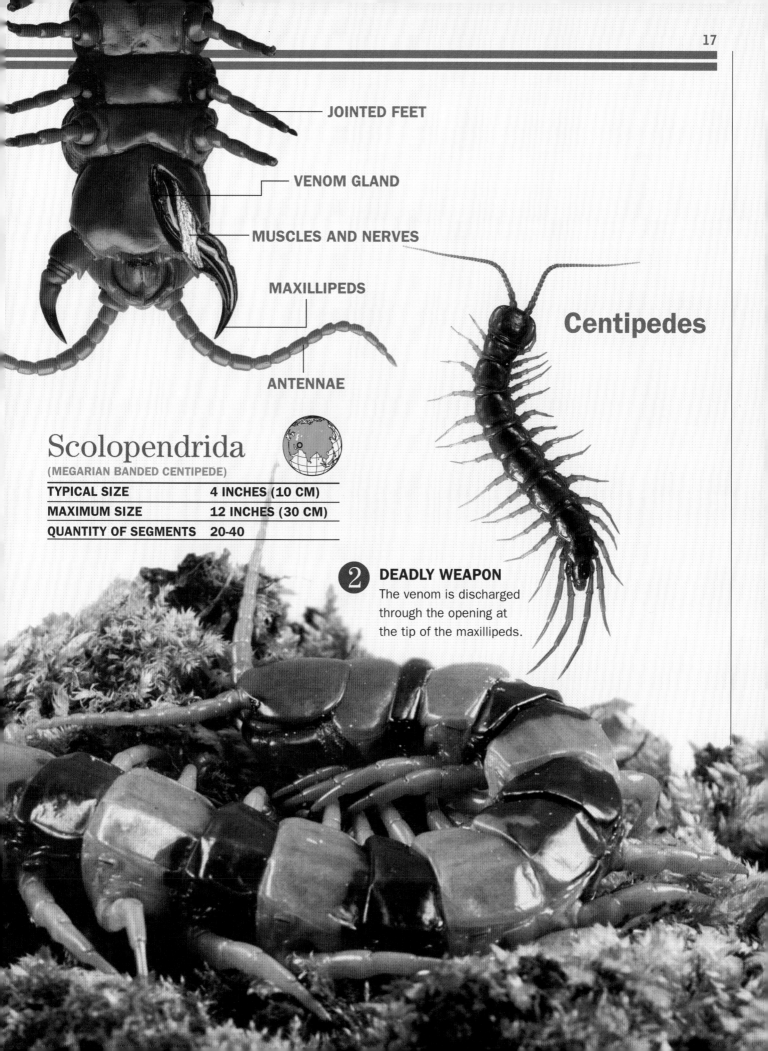

The Art of Flying

One of the most basic adaptations of insects has been their ability to fly. Most have two pairs of wings. Beetles use one pair to fly and one pair for protection. The front pair of wings used for protection are called elytra.

The vertical muscle contracts and the wings move upward.

Thorax

Wing

The horizontal muscle contracts and the wings move downward.

"Ladies" of Land and Air

Some 4,500 species of these beetles live throughout the world. Almost all are brightly colored, with black spots on a red, yellow, or orange background.

IDENTIFYING SPOTS

7 BLACK
SPOTS

③ FLIGHT

Raised
elytra

40-80 inches per second
(1-2 m/s)
AVERAGE SPEED OF FLIGHT

② TAKEOFF

Wings prepared
for flight

① PREPARATION

ELYTRON

Raised
elytron

Visible
wing

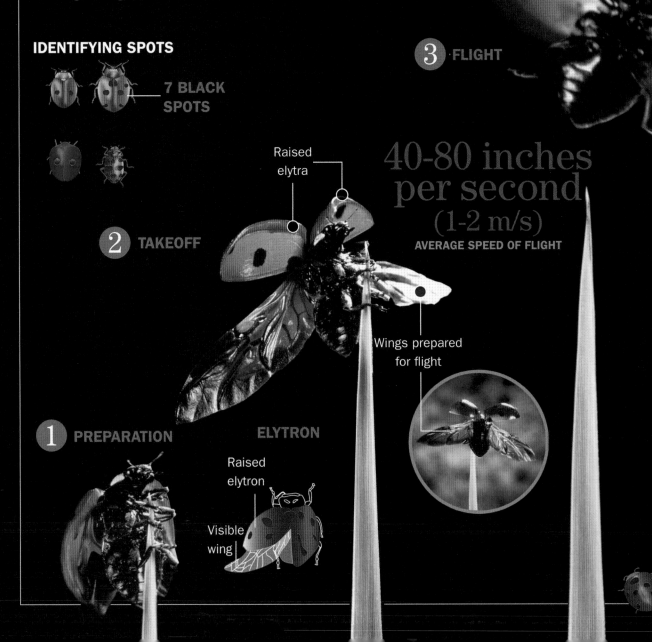

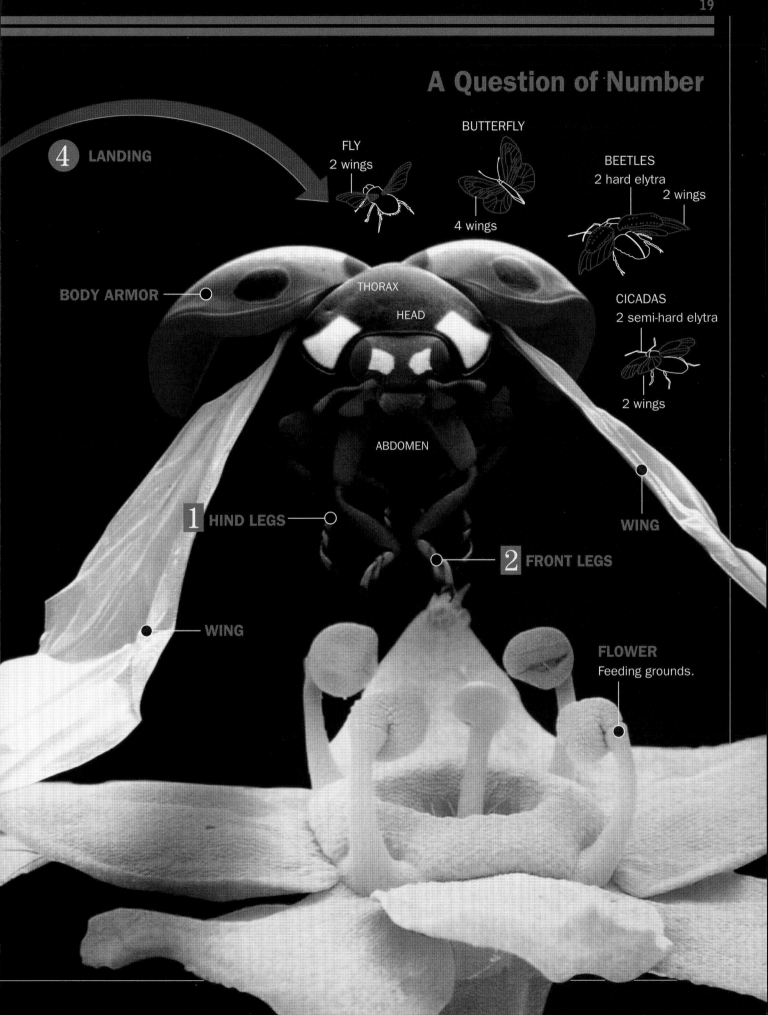

A Question of Number

FLY
2 wings

BUTTERFLY
4 wings

BEETLES
2 hard elytra
2 wings

CICADAS
2 semi-hard elytra
2 wings

4 LANDING

BODY ARMOR

THORAX
HEAD

ABDOMEN

1 HIND LEGS

2 FRONT LEGS

WING

WING

FLOWER
Feeding grounds.

Order and Progress

Ants are one of the insects with the highest social organization. In the *colony*, each inhabitant has a job to do. The head of the family is the queen, the only one that reproduces. All the rest of the ants are her offspring.

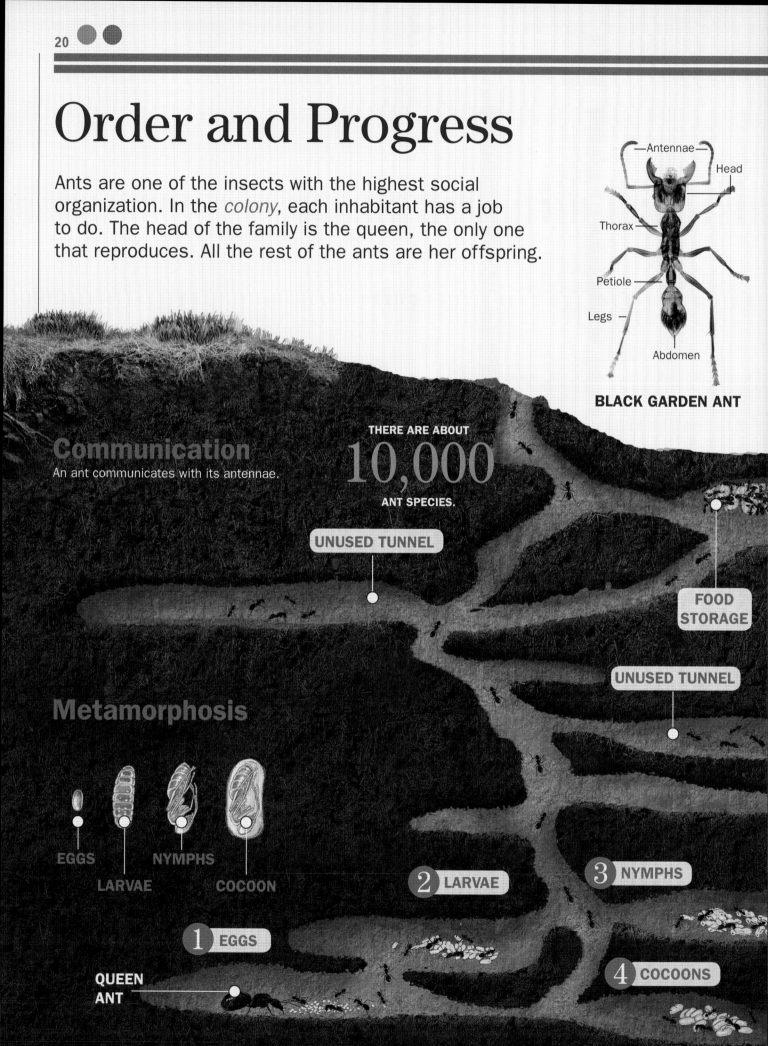

Antennae

Head

Thorax

Petiole

Legs

Abdomen

BLACK GARDEN ANT

Communication

An ant communicates with its antennae.

THERE ARE ABOUT

10,000

ANT SPECIES.

UNUSED TUNNEL

FOOD STORAGE

UNUSED TUNNEL

Metamorphosis

EGGS

NYMPHS

LARVAE

COCOON

2 LARVAE

3 NYMPHS

1 EGGS

QUEEN ANT

4 COCOONS

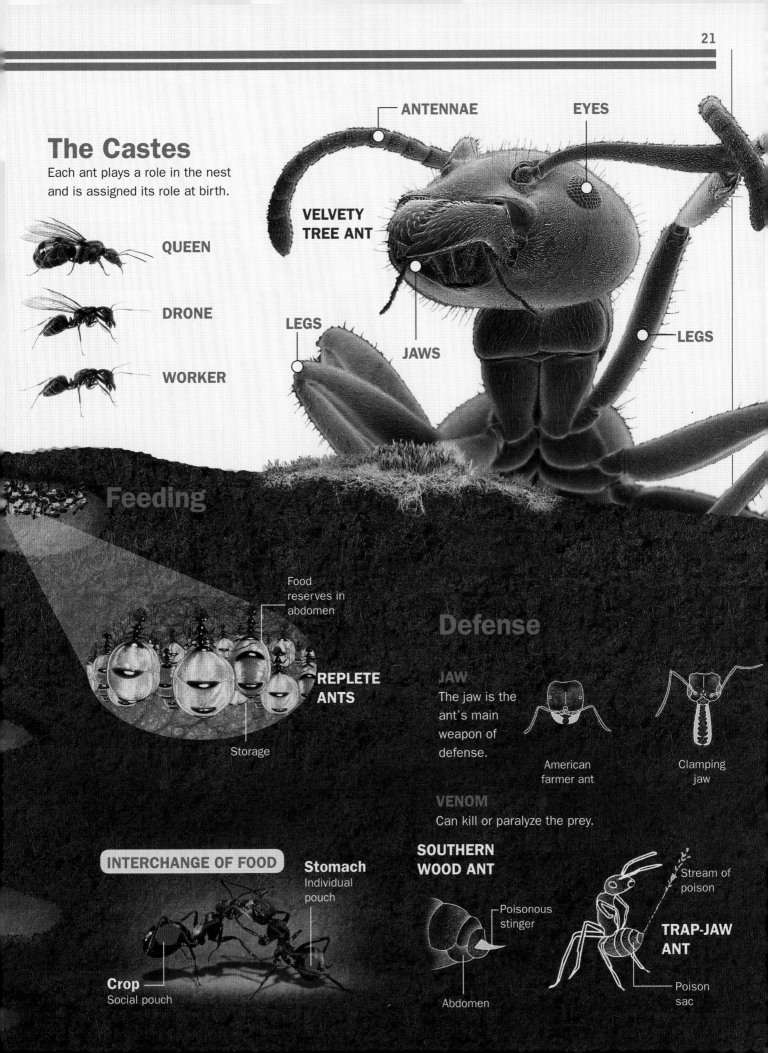

The Castes

Each ant plays a role in the nest and is assigned its role at birth.

QUEEN

DRONE

WORKER

ANTENNAE

EYES

VELVETY TREE ANT

LEGS

JAWS

LEGS

Feeding

Food reserves in abdomen

REPLETE ANTS

Storage

Defense

JAW

The jaw is the ant's main weapon of defense.

American farmer ant

Clamping jaw

VENOM

Can kill or paralyze the prey.

SOUTHERN WOOD ANT

Poisonous stinger

Abdomen

Stream of poison

TRAP-JAW ANT

Poison sac

INTERCHANGE OF FOOD

Stomach
Individual pouch

Crop
Social pouch

Metamorphosis

Metamorphosis is the change in shape that insects undergo as they grow. There are two types of transformations: complete, like that of monarch butterflies, and incomplete, like that of dragonflies or grasshoppers. Insects with complete metamorphosis pass through a pupal, or chrysalid, phase.

① IN THE BEGINNING, THE EGG

7 days

**AMOUNT OF TIME THE LARVA
LIVES INSIDE THE EGG**

FIVE CHANGES
When it hatches, the insect is shaped like a worm. This caterpillar will molt its exoskeleton five times as it grows in size.

CHANGE TO PUPAL PHASE

HATCHING

FOURTH SHEDDING

SECOND SHEDDING

THIRD SHEDDING

EMPEROR DRAGONFLY

③ IMAGO (ADULT)

SIMPLE METAMORPHOSIS
Simple, or incomplete, metamorphosis does not include a pupal phase.

① EGG

② NYMPH

❷ LARVA OR CATERPILLAR

3 weeks
IS THE AMOUNT OF TIME THE INSECT LIVES IN THE LARVAL STAGE.

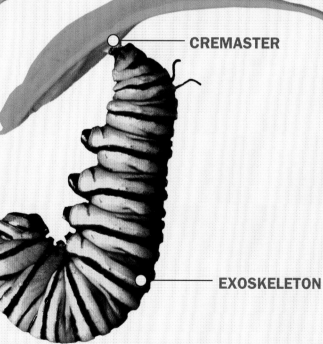

CREMASTER

EXOSKELETON

PREPARATION FOR THE PUPAL PHASE
A greenish tissue will form the cocoon, or chrysalis.

INSIDE THE LARVA

INTESTINE

15 DAYS

LENGTH OF THE PUPA, OR CHRYSALIS, PHASE

❸ PUPA (CHRYSALIS)

After getting rid of its larval exoskeleton, the insect hangs from a branch, protected by a cocoon.

CAMOUFLAGE

The chrysalid capsule has shapes, textures, and colors that help keep it from being noticed, to protect it from predators. The capsules typically resemble leaves or bird droppings.

INTERNAL ORGANS

The Time Draws Near

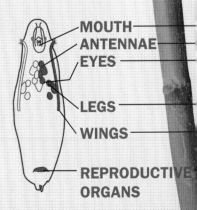

MOUTH
ANTENNAE
EYES
LEGS
WINGS
REPRODUCTIVE ORGANS

④ ADULT

1 **2** **3**

Fly Away, Butterfly

YOUNG ADULT

Anatomy of a Butterfly

Goal: Survival

Some insects, *camouflaged* as branches or leaves, can escape notice so as to hunt or to hide from predators. To avoid being attacked, other insects develop colors and shapes that deceive other animals and keep them from attacking.

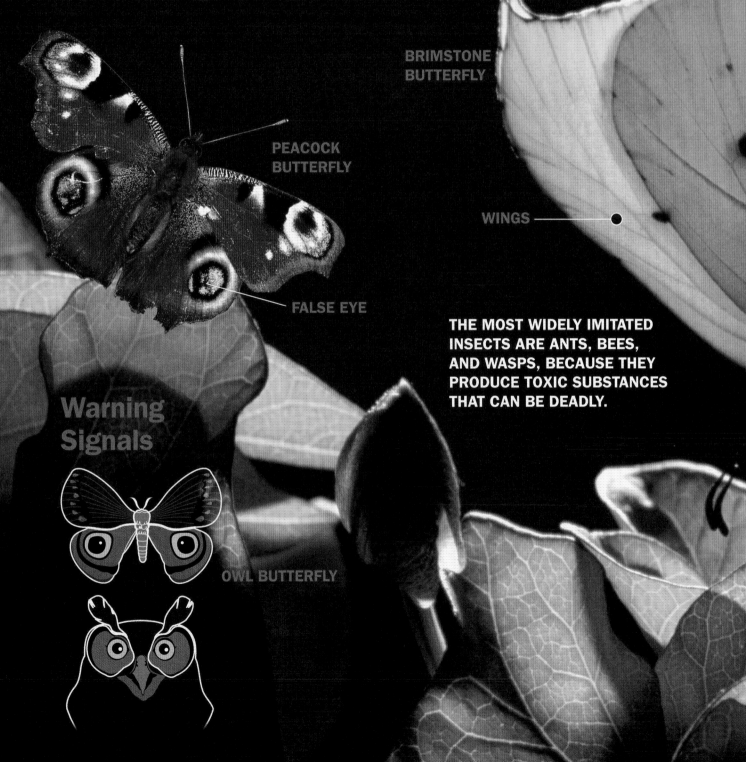

BRIMSTONE BUTTERFLY

PEACOCK BUTTERFLY

WINGS

FALSE EYE

THE MOST WIDELY IMITATED INSECTS ARE ANTS, BEES, AND WASPS, BECAUSE THEY PRODUCE TOXIC SUBSTANCES THAT CAN BE DEADLY.

Warning Signals

OWL BUTTERFLY

BODY

AUSTRALIAN STICK INSECT

LEGS

VEINS

EYES

THISTLE MANTIS

FRONT LEGS

Distant Kin

The first amphibians evolved from fish with fleshy, lobed fins that resembled legs. During long droughts, the fish used their fleshy fins to move from one pond to another. Oxygen availability was also affected, and this led to more organisms being able to breathe oxygen from the air. The first four-legged animals had no competition on land.

Legs Evolved in the Water.

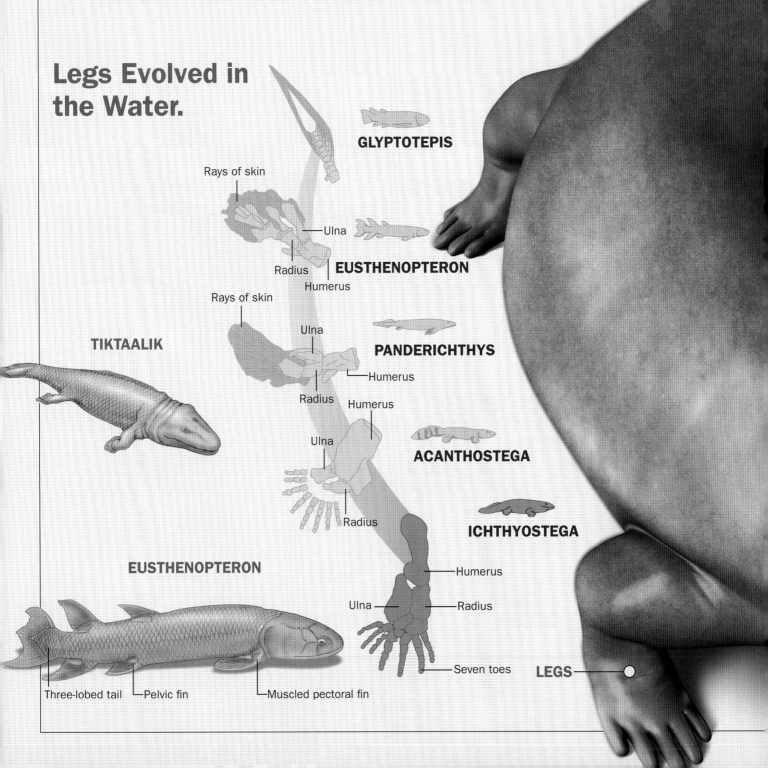

GLYPTOTEPIS

Rays of skin

Ulna

EUSTHENOPTERON

Radius

Humerus

Rays of skin

TIKTAALIK

Ulna

PANDERICHTHYS

Humerus

Radius

Humerus

Ulna

ACANTHOSTEGA

Radius

ICHTHYOSTEGA

EUSTHENOPTERON

Humerus

Ulna — Radius

Three-lobed tail — Pelvic fin — Muscled pectoral fin

Seven toes — LEGS

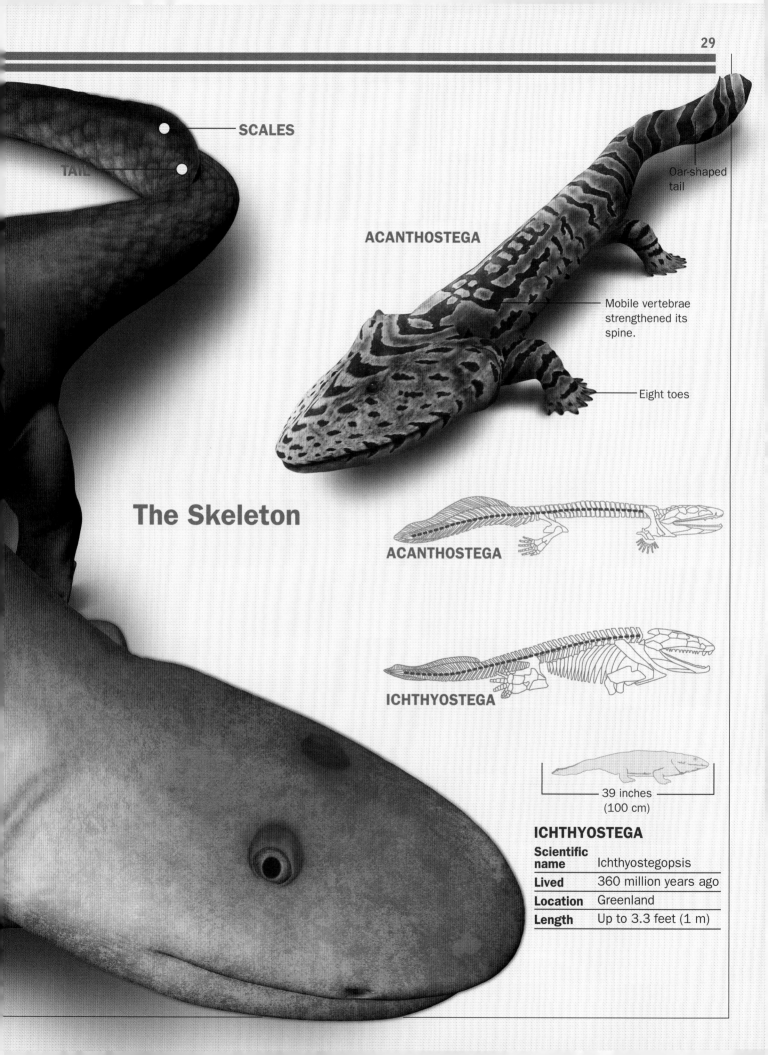

SCALES

TAIL

ACANTHOSTEGA

Oar-shaped tail

Mobile vertebrae strengthened its spine.

Eight toes

The Skeleton

ACANTHOSTEGA

ICHTHYOSTEGA

39 inches (100 cm)

ICHTHYOSTEGA

Scientific name	Ichthyostegopsis
Lived	360 million years ago
Location	Greenland
Length	Up to 3.3 feet (1 m)

Between Land and Water

As their name (*amphi*, "both," and *bios*, "life") says, these animals lead a double life. When young, they live in the water, and when they become adults they live outside it. However, many must remain near water or in very humid places to keep from drying out. Amphibians also breathe through their skin, and only moist skin can absorb oxygen.

Amphibian Anatomy

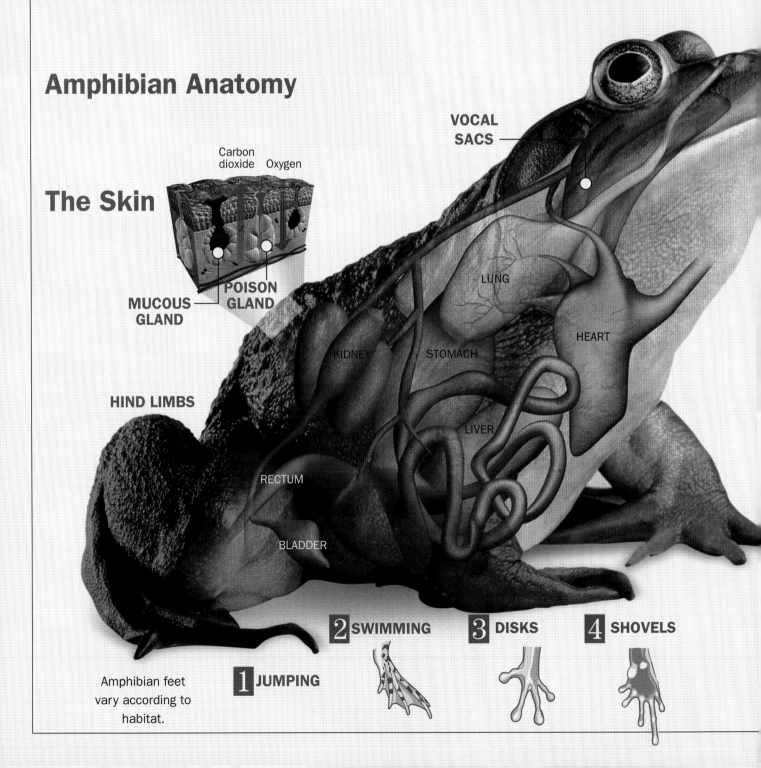

The Skin

Carbon dioxide Oxygen

MUCOUS GLAND

POISON GLAND

VOCAL SACS

LUNG

HEART

KIDNEY

STOMACH

LIVER

HIND LIMBS

RECTUM

BLADDER

Amphibian feet vary according to habitat.

1 JUMPING

2 SWIMMING

3 DISKS

4 SHOVELS

Difference Between Frogs and Toads

SKIN

REED FROG

LEGS

SKIN

LEGS

COMMON TOAD

CATCHING

Nutrition

is based on plants during the larval stage. Adults eat arthropods and other invertebrates.

Types of Amphibians

1 ANURA

EUROPEAN TREE FROG

2 APODA

RINGED CAECILIAN

TIGER SALAMANDER

3 URODELA

Jumping Athletes

Frogs and toads are known for their ability to jump high and far. Frogs use their jumping ability to escape from their many predators; they can jump a distance equivalent to 10 to 44 times their body length.

2 FEEDING

VISIBLE HUMP

STRETCHED-OUT BODY

1 JUMPING

EDIBLE FROG

LEG MUSCLES

HIND FEET

ASIAN TREE FROG

HOW IT FEEDS

1 ADHESION

EYES

2 NO ESCAPE

FOREFEET

3 FALL

WHITE-LIPPED TREE FROG

The toe has a sticky mucous coating.

NINE VERTEBRAE

17.5 feet
(5.35 m)
THE DISTANCE JUMPED BY AN AFRICAN FROG

THE TOAD'S JUMP

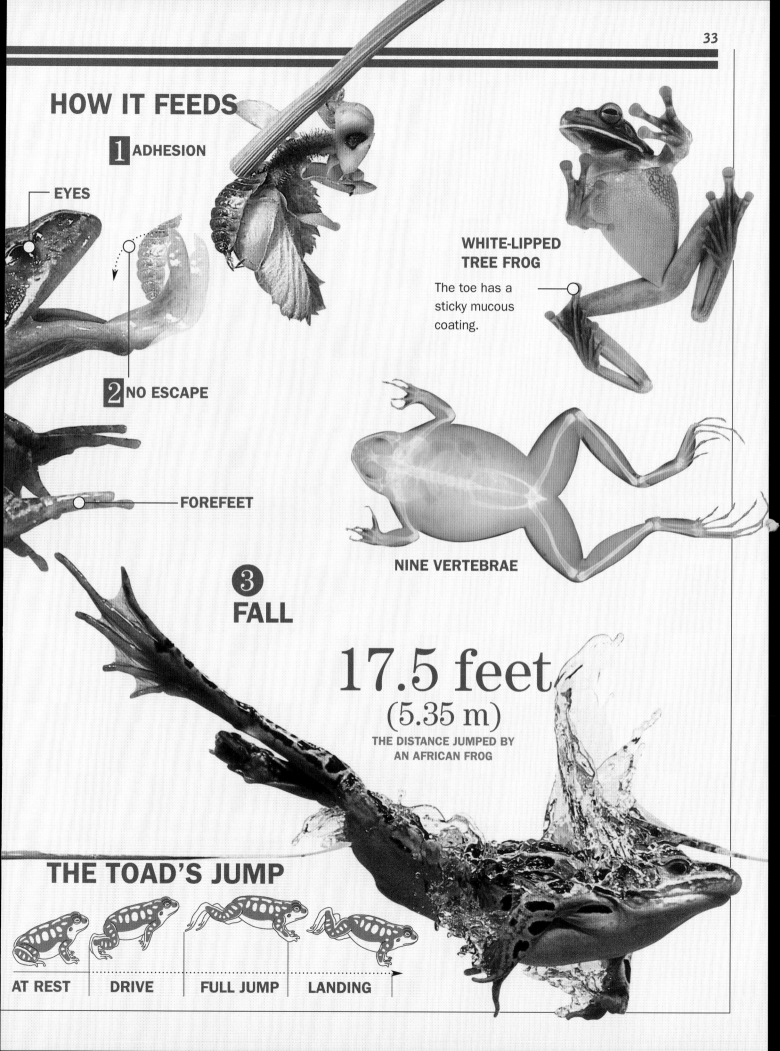

| AT REST | DRIVE | FULL JUMP | LANDING |

Poison in Color

Not all that glitters is gold, nor is it healthy. The skin of some amphibians has glands that *secrete* poison. Color is a warning sign, a way of keeping possible attackers away, and also a way to defend territory during mating season.

WARNING COLOR BANDS

Poisoned Darts

1 TADPOLE

ABOUT

3,600

SPECIES OF AMPHIBIANS
RECORDED IN THE WORLD
ARE POISONOUS.

2 TADPOLE WITH LEGS

SALAMANDERS

3 ADULT

GLAND

EYE

STRONG HIND LEGS

GLAND

MOIST SKIN

MARBLED SALAMANDER

LONG TAIL

SOFT FEET

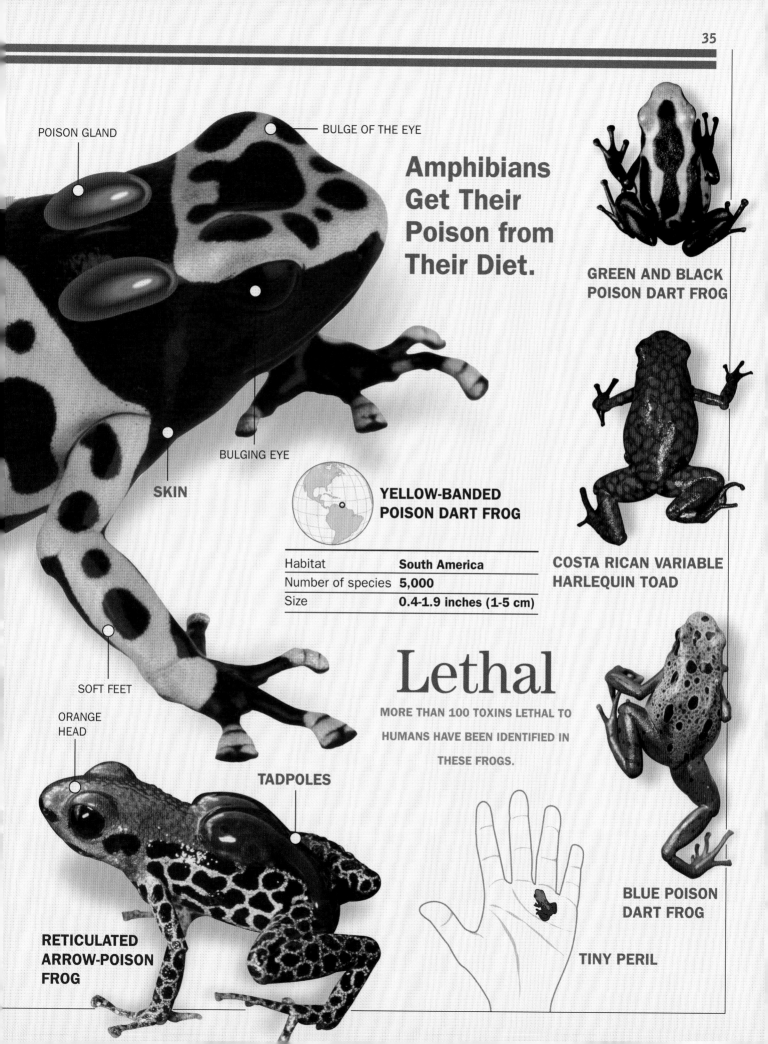

POISON GLAND

BULGE OF THE EYE

Amphibians Get Their Poison from Their Diet.

GREEN AND BLACK POISON DART FROG

BULGING EYE

SKIN

YELLOW-BANDED POISON DART FROG

Habitat	South America
Number of species	5,000
Size	0.4-1.9 inches (1-5 cm)

COSTA RICAN VARIABLE HARLEQUIN TOAD

SOFT FEET

ORANGE HEAD

TADPOLES

Lethal

MORE THAN 100 TOXINS LETHAL TO HUMANS HAVE BEEN IDENTIFIED IN THESE FROGS.

BLUE POISON DART FROG

RETICULATED ARROW-POISON FROG

TINY PERIL

Newts and Salamanders

Newts and salamanders are the most primitive of terrestrial vertebrates. Newts closely resemble the animals from which all amphibians are descended. Unlike frogs and toads, newts and salamanders keep their tails as adults. They are found in *temperate* regions of the Northern Hemisphere.

The Salamander Life Cycle

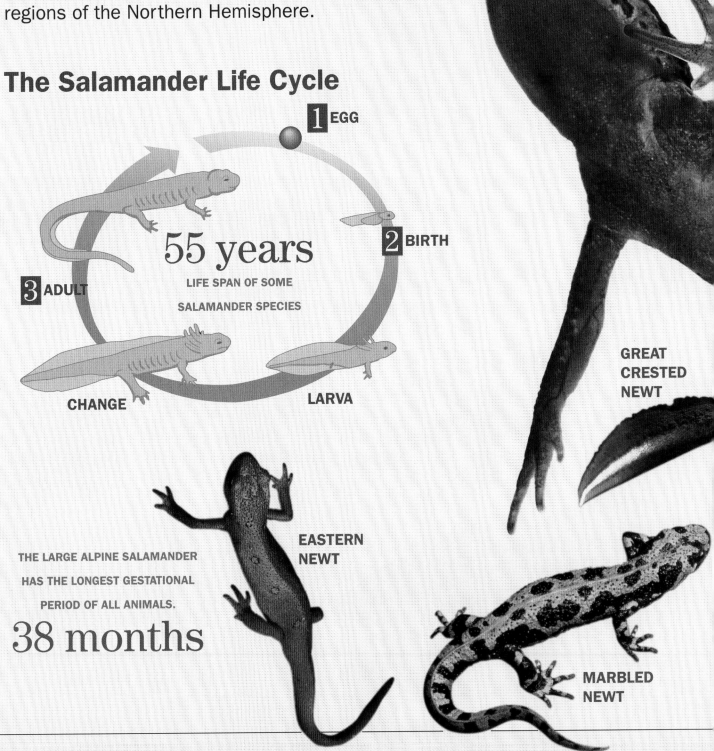

1 EGG

2 BIRTH

3 ADMIN → ADULT

55 years
LIFE SPAN OF SOME SALAMANDER SPECIES

CHANGE

LARVA

FRONT FEET

GREAT CRESTED NEWT

EASTERN NEWT

THE LARGE ALPINE SALAMANDER HAS THE LONGEST GESTATIONAL PERIOD OF ALL ANIMALS.

38 months

MARBLED NEWT

Anatomy of a Newt

TAIL

PALMATE NEWT

Feeding

BELLY

HIND FEET

Male's crest

Newts and Water

SMOOTH
NEWT

Land of Mammals

After the *extinction* of the large dinosaurs at the end of the Mesozoic Era, mammals found the opportunity to evolve. Within the zoological class of mammals, *primates* appeared, as did the immediate ancestors of humans toward the end of the era.

CONTINENTS OF THE PAST

PRESENT-DAY CONTINENTS

200 million years
MAMMALS HAVE BEEN ON LAND

THE CLASS THAT DEFINES AN ERA
Some 220 million years ago, the earliest mammals appeared, which today are all extinct. 100 million years ago, the two predominant surviving suborders appeared— the *marsupials* and the *placentals*.

Ancestors of Humans

MORGANUCODON
An early rodent

SHORT TAIL

THEROPITHECUS OSWALDI

COMPARATIVE SIZE

COMPARATIVE SIZE

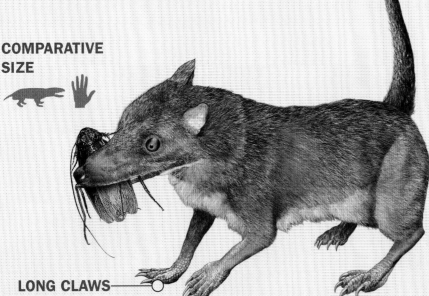

PREHENSILE THUMB

LONG CLAWS

PALEOGENE
65.5 TO 23 MILLION YEARS AGO

Includes the Paleocene, Eocene, and Oligocene epochs.

NEOGENE
23 MILLION YEARS AGO TO 1.8 MILLION YEARS AGO

Includes the Miocene and Pliocene epochs.

New Plants

TAIL
They used it for balance while climbing.

**SYCAMORE
(PALEOCENE)**

**FICUS
(EOCENE)**

**GRASSES
(PLIOCENE)**

60
million
years ago
SINCE THE APPEARANCE OF
PRIMATES ON EARTH

**SPRUCE
(PLEISTOCENE)**

LONG FINGERS

**RANUNCULUS
(PLEISTOCENE)**

**PLEISTOCENE
FROM 1.8 MILLION TO
12,000 YEARS AGO**

**HOLOCENE
FROM 12,000 YEARS AGO TO THE PRESENT**

Names and Groups

The mammals class is divided into two subclasses: Prototheria, which lay eggs, and Theria. The Theria, in turn, are divided into two infraclasses— Metatheria (*marsupials*), which grow to viability within a marsupium, or pouch, and Eutheria (*placental mammals*), whose offspring are born completely developed and who today represent the great majority of living mammal species.

ECHIDNA

Prototheria
ORDER MONOTREMATA
The only living representatives of this order are echidnas and the platypus.

CURRENTLY

4

**ECHIDNA
SPECIES KNOWN**

HORNY BEAK

—— FINS

—— PLATYPUS

GEOGRAPHICALLY CONFINED
Platypuses and echidnas are found only in Oceania.

—— AUSTRALIA

Theria
INFRACLASS METATHERIA
Marsupials live in the mother's
pouch until they completely develop.

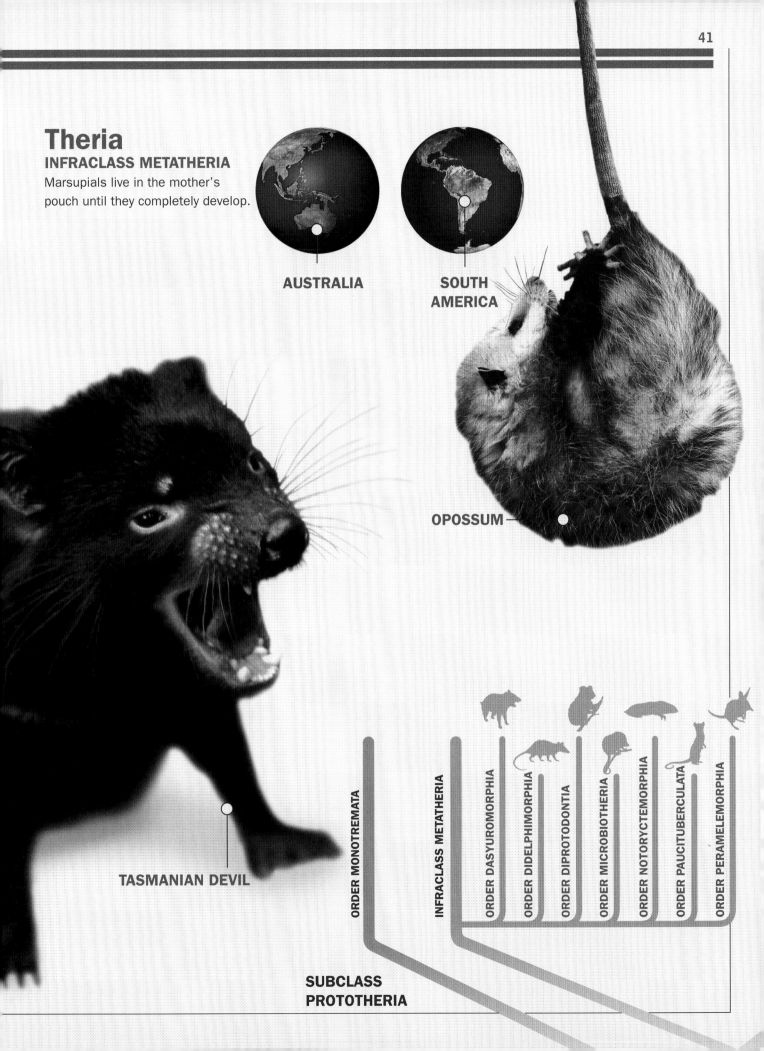

AUSTRALIA

**SOUTH
AMERICA**

OPOSSUM

TASMANIAN DEVIL

ORDER MONOTREMATA

INFRACLASS METATHERIA

ORDER DASYUROMORPHIA

ORDER DIDELPHIMORPHIA

ORDER DIPROTODONTIA

ORDER MICROBIOTHERIA

ORDER NOTORYCTEMORPHIA

ORDER PAUCITUBERCULATA

ORDER PERAMELEMORPHIA

**SUBCLASS
PROTOTHERIA**

Infraclass Eutheria

Commonly called placental mammals, they are the typical mammals. They probably began diversifying during the Cretaceous Period (65-150 million years ago).

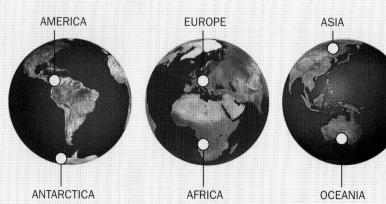

AMERICA
EUROPE
ASIA
ANTARCTICA
AFRICA
OCEANIA

Throughout the World

The eutherians, or placental mammals, are the most important group of mammals because of the number of living species they represent.

RACCOON
Order Carnivora

JURASSIC BEAVER
This beaver lived in China 140 million years ago.

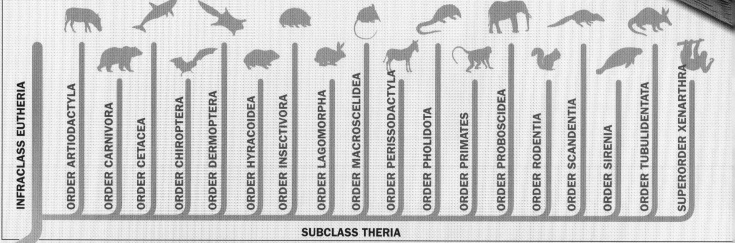

INFRACLASS EUTHERIA

ORDER ARTIODACTYLA

ORDER CARNIVORA

ORDER CETACEA

ORDER CHIROPTERA

ORDER DERMOPTERA

ORDER HYRACOIDEA

ORDER INSECTIVORA

ORDER LAGOMORPHA

ORDER MACROSCELIDEA

ORDER PERISSODACTYLA

ORDER PHOLIDOTA

ORDER PRIMATES

ORDER PROBOSCIDEA

ORDER RODENTIA

ORDER SCANDENTIA

ORDER SIRENIA

ORDER TUBULIDENTATA

SUPERORDER XENARTHRA

SUBCLASS THERIA

GIRAFFE
Order Artyodactilae

NECK

SEAL
Order Carnivora

SKIN

MANDRILL
Order Primates

What Is a Mammal?

Mammals share a series of characteristics that distinguish their class: a body covered by hair, the birth of live young, and the feeding of newborns on milk produced by the females' *mammary glands*. All breathe through lungs. The ability to maintain a constant body temperature has allowed them to spread out and conquer every corner of the Earth.

A Body for Every Environment

BOTTLENOSE DOLPHIN

HAIR
Body hair is unique to mammals and absent in other classes of animals.

TEETH

CHIPMUNK

Close Relatives

Humans belong to the primate group. Hominids (orangutans, gorillas, and chimpanzees) are the largest of these, weighing between 105 and 595 pounds (48-270 kg).

Homeothermy

The ability to keep body temperature relatively constant, independent of the ambient temperature.

ALWAYS 98° F (37° C)

CRANIUM

AN EAR OF BONES

LOWER JAW

MAMMARY GLANDS

GORILLA

GRIZZLY BEAR (BROWN BEAR)

LIMBS
Mammals usually have four limbs.

ELEPHANT SEAL

Take Habitat into Account

Aquatic	Temperate Forests	Desert	Meadow or Pastureland

Tropical Savanna	Tropical Rainforest	Taiga	Tundra

A THICK SKIN

Life Cycle

Birth, maturity, reproduction, and death: this life cycle has certain particularities among mammals. As a general rule, the larger a mammal, the longer the members of its species tend to live but the fewer offspring are born to a single female per *litter* or reproductive season.

90 Years
A WHALE'S AVERAGE LIFE SPAN

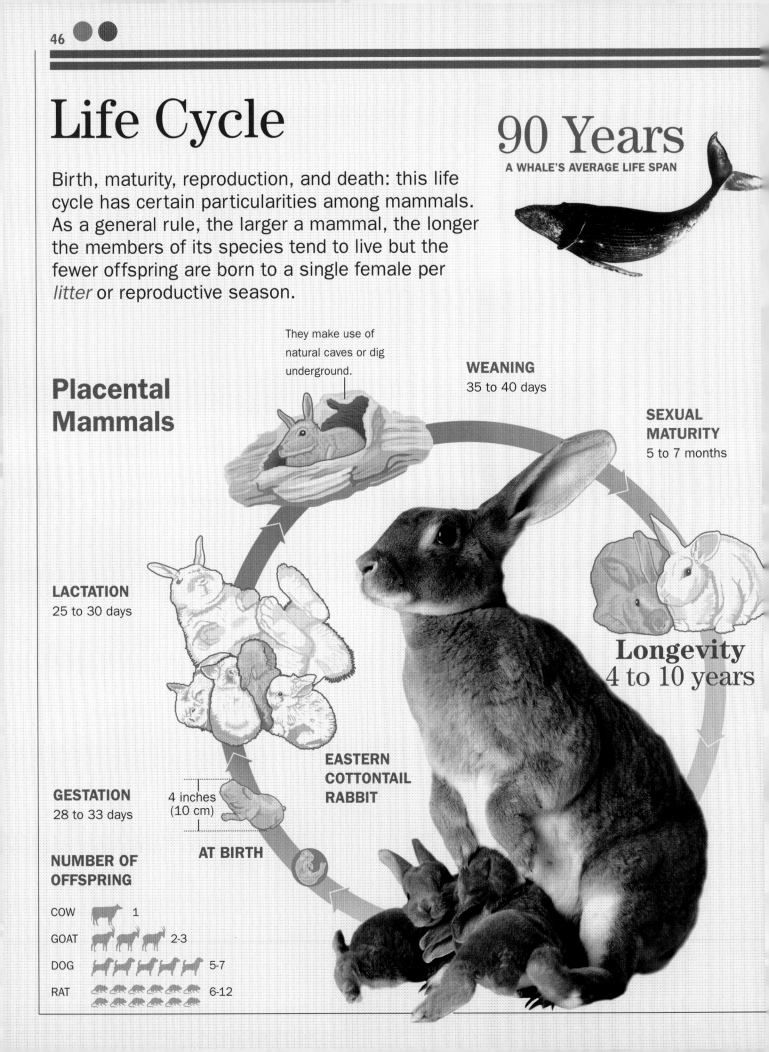

Placental Mammals

They make use of natural caves or dig underground.

WEANING
35 to 40 days

SEXUAL MATURITY
5 to 7 months

Longevity
4 to 10 years

LACTATION
25 to 30 days

EASTERN COTTONTAIL RABBIT

GESTATION
28 to 33 days

4 inches (10 cm)

AT BIRTH

NUMBER OF OFFSPRING

COW		1
GOAT		2-3
DOG		5-7
RAT		6-12

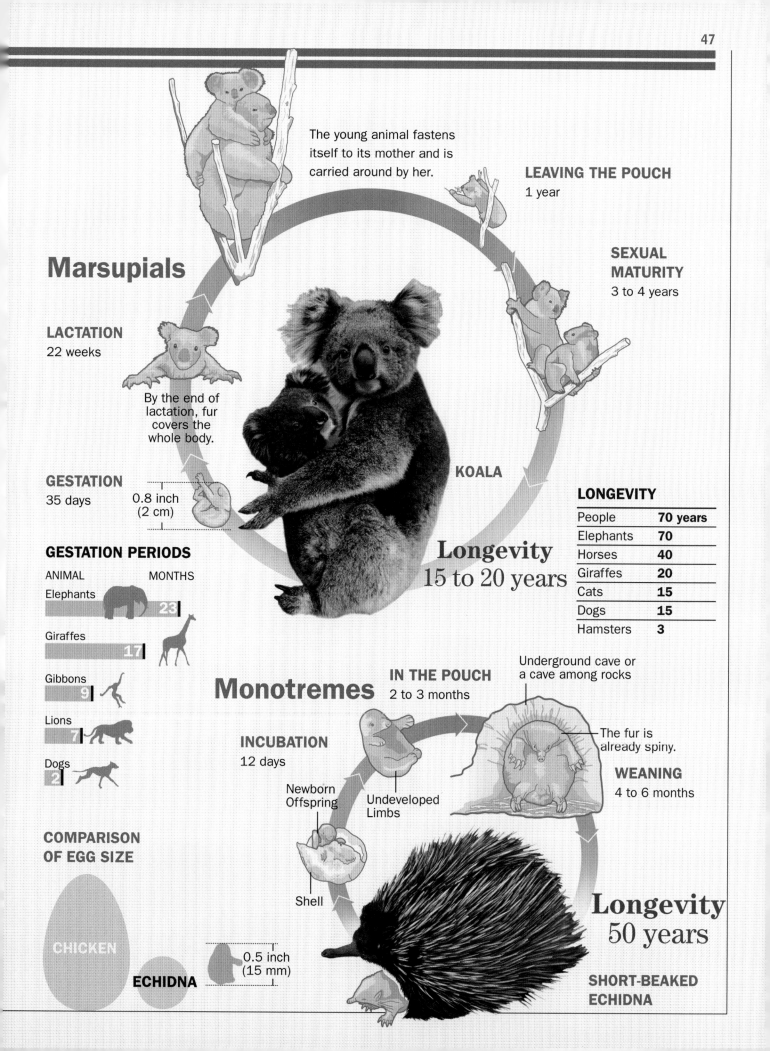

Marsupials

The young animal fastens itself to its mother and is carried around by her.

LEAVING THE POUCH
1 year

SEXUAL MATURITY
3 to 4 years

LACTATION
22 weeks

By the end of lactation, fur covers the whole body.

GESTATION
35 days

0.8 inch
(2 cm)

KOALA

Longevity
15 to 20 years

GESTATION PERIODS

ANIMAL	MONTHS
Elephants	23
Giraffes	17
Gibbons	9
Lions	7
Dogs	2

LONGEVITY

People	**70 years**
Elephants	**70**
Horses	**40**
Giraffes	**20**
Cats	**15**
Dogs	**15**
Hamsters	**3**

Monotremes

IN THE POUCH
2 to 3 months

Underground cave or a cave among rocks

The fur is already spiny.

INCUBATION
12 days

WEANING
4 to 6 months

Newborn Offspring

Undeveloped Limbs

Shell

COMPARISON OF EGG SIZE

CHICKEN

ECHIDNA

0.5 inch
(15 mm)

Longevity
50 years

SHORT-BEAKED ECHIDNA

Development and Growth

Play is much more than entertainment for young mammals. It is the way in which they learn to be part of their species in the early stages of their lives, simultaneously acquiring the basic means of survival. In their games, chimpanzees perform primary instinctive activities that, with time and improvement, will become perfected instinctive activities. These include using tools, balancing in trees, and forming communication.

OVER
15
TYPES OF CALLS ARE EMITTED BY CHIMPANZEES.

This expression communicates terror.

This expression transmits submission.

This gesture indicates worry.

Communication

GAMES
Play appears to be limited to mammals.

SOCIAL RELATIONS
Play helps encourage apes to identify with their species.

SURVIVAL

Play functions as a method of learning to survive in a wild habitat.

EXTREMITIES

Chimpanzees are characterized by their long arms, which have great strength, and by their opposable thumbs.

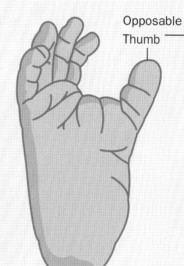

Opposable Thumb

Long Digits

Use of Tools

words

THEY CAN LEARN AND EXPRESS WORDS USING SIGN LANGUAGE.

A chimpanzee pokes a stump in search of termites, using a stick as a tool.

A LIFE OF HANGING

Soft Contact

Admired, adored, and coveted by humans, a mammal's fur coat is much more than a skin covering. It acts as a protective layer against injuries, prevents invasion by germs, and regulates the loss of body heat and moisture. In many species, it provides *camouflage* by changing color and texture from winter to summer.

FUR AND MIMICRY

Mammals from cold regions, such as polar bears, have white fur to camouflage themselves in snow. Others change their fur color with the seasons.

WINTER

SUMMER

UV

FUR SERVES TO PROTECT THE SKIN FROM EXCESSIVE UV RAYS.

THE SKIN

EPIDERMIS

DERMIS

FATTY TISSUE

SWEAT GLANDS

HAIR SHAFT

SWEAT PORE

FOLLICL

ARTERY

VEIN

GREY WOLF

HARE

CHINCHILLA

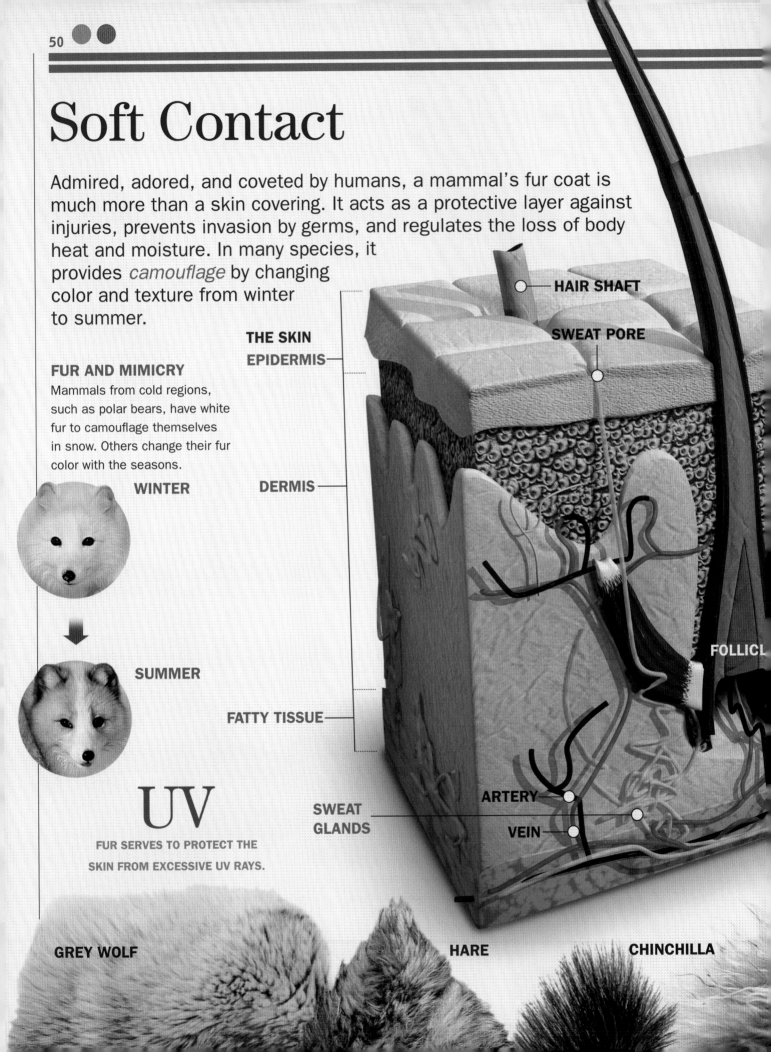

HAIR STRUCTURE

Diverse Hairs

BAT HAIR

WOOL FIBER

POLAR BEAR HAIR

PORCUPINE QUILLS

Mini-quills

DERMAL PAPILLA

MERKEL'S DISK

SEBACEOUS GLAND

Insulating Skin

OUTER FUR

PACINIAN CORPUSCLE

UNDERFUR

LAYER OF FAT

30,000

THE NUMBER OF QUILLS THAT COVER A PORCUPINE

PORCUPINE

SEA LION (JUVENILE)

MACAQUE MONKEY

COATI

Constant Heat

Mammals are homeothermic—which means they are capable of maintaining a stable internal body temperature despite environmental conditions. This ability has allowed them to establish themselves in every region of the planet.

A PERFECT SYSTEM
Polar bears, like all mammals, keep their internal temperature constant.

Great Swimmers

POLAR BEAR

Sheltered Cubs

Metabolism

Migration

WHEN SPRING BEGINS, THESE BEARS TRAVEL SOUTH, ESCAPING THE BREAKUP OF THE ARCTIC ICE.

RESPIRATORY PATHWAYS
The bears have membranes in their snouts that warm and humidify the air before it reaches the lungs.

Under the Ice

Hollow chamber with air

HAIR

Surface

SECONDARY ACCESS TUNNEL

CHAMBER OF REFUGE

MAIN ACCESS TUNNEL

ENTRANCE

GUARD HAIRS

UNDERFUR

FAT

PRINCIPAL FAT PRESERVES

Curling Up

OVER

6 miles (10 km)

PER HOUR IS THE AVERAGE SPEED AT WHICH POLAR BEARS SWIM.

Slow and Steady Swimmers

HIND LEGS

FORELIMBS

THE FLOATING SLAB

TO GET OUT: ANTISLIP PALMS

Extremities

Mammals' extremities are modified according to the way in which each species moves about. Thus, for example, they become fins for swimming in aquatic mammals and wings in bats. In land mammals, these variations depend on the way the animal bears its weight in walking.

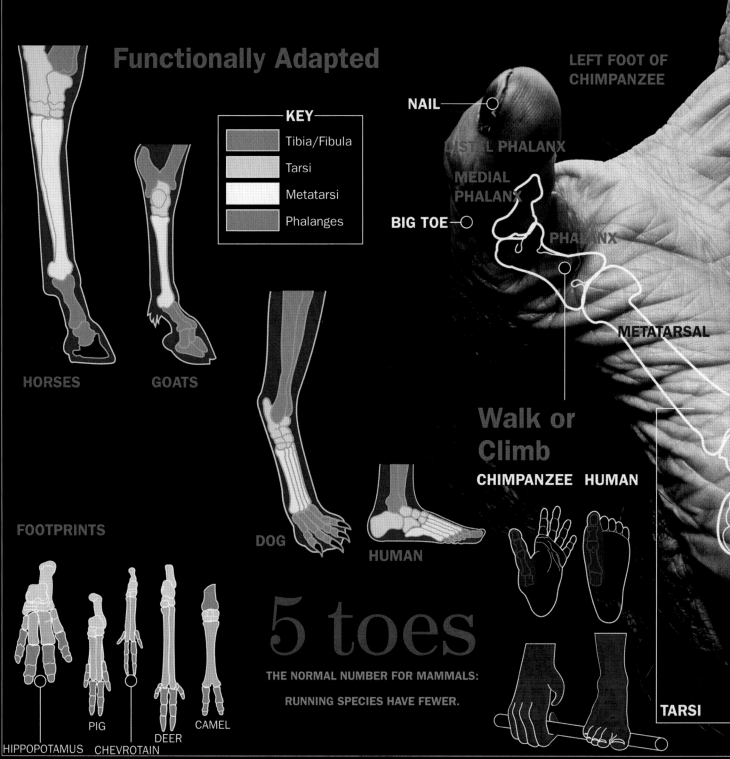

Functionally Adapted

KEY

	Tibia/Fibula
	Tarsi
	Metatarsi
	Phalanges

HORSES   GOATS

FOOTPRINTS

DOG

HUMAN

LEFT FOOT OF CHIMPANZEE

NAIL

DISTAL PHALANX

MEDIAL PHALANX

BIG TOE

PHALANX

METATARSAL

Walk or Climb

CHIMPANZEE HUMAN

TARSI

5 toes

THE NORMAL NUMBER FOR MAMMALS:

RUNNING SPECIES HAVE FEWER.

HIPPOPOTAMUS   CHEVROTAIN   PIG   DEER   CAMEL

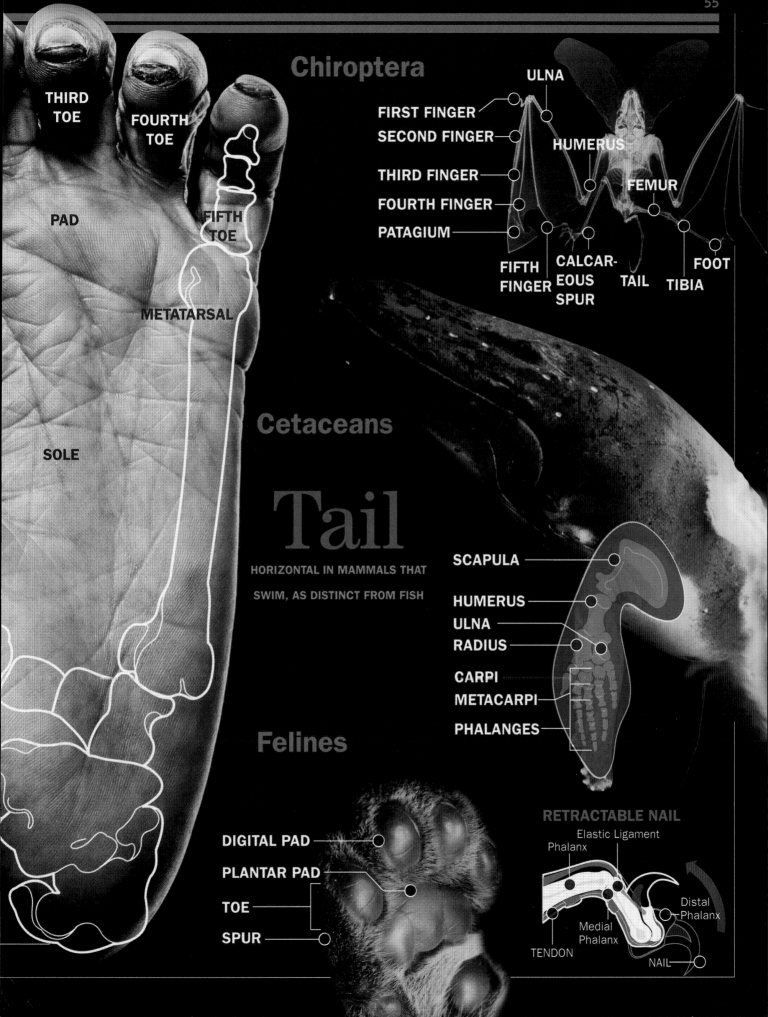

THIRD TOE

FOURTH TOE

PAD

FIFTH TOE

METATARSAL

SOLE

Chiroptera

ULNA

FIRST FINGER

SECOND FINGER

HUMERUS

THIRD FINGER

FOURTH FINGER

FEMUR

PATAGIUM

FIFTH FINGER

CALCAR-EOUS SPUR

TAIL

TIBIA

FOOT

Cetaceans

Tail

HORIZONTAL IN MAMMALS THAT SWIM, AS DISTINCT FROM FISH

SCAPULA

HUMERUS

ULNA

RADIUS

CARPI

METACARPI

PHALANGES

Felines

DIGITAL PAD

PLANTAR PAD

TOE

SPUR

RETRACTABLE NAIL

Elastic Ligament

Phalanx

Distal Phalanx

Medial Phalanx

TENDON

NAIL

Of Flesh Thou Art

The *carnivore* group is composed of species whose diet is based on hunting other animals. Lions, the most sociable of the *felines*, have good vision and sharp hearing; they live in packs, and when they go hunting, they do so as a group.

Lions

Teeth

The Hunt

UPPER PREMOLARS

UPPER CANINE

UPPER INCISORS

1 LYING IN AMBUSH

ANTERIOR PREMOLARS

LOWER INCISORS

CARNASSIAL MOLAR

LOWER CANINE

Family	Felidae
Species	*Panthera leo*
Weight	265-410 pounds (120-185 kg)

Size (female)

9 feet (2.7 m)
3 feet (1 m)

Main Prey

BUFFALO **ZEBRA** **GIRAFFE**

GNU **GAZELLE** **ANTELOPE**

SIGHT COAT

THE TAIL

40 pounds (18 kg)

OF MEAT CAN BE EATEN BY A LION IN A SINGLE MEAL.

2 ACCELERATION   3 LEAP   4 LETHAL BITE

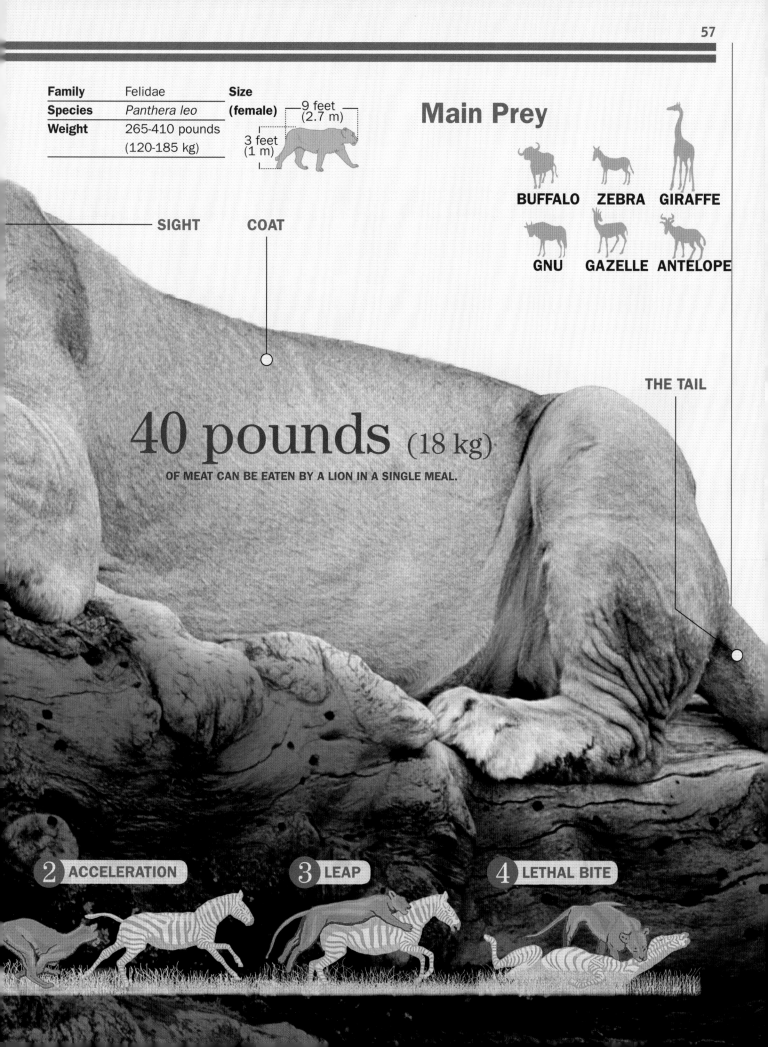

Herbivores

Ruminants, such as cows, sheep, or camels, have stomachs made of multiple chambers. They need to eat large quantities of grass in very short times, so they have developed a digestive system that allows them to swallow food, store it, and then return it to the mouth to chew calmly.

8
HOURS OF RUMINATION DAILY

40 gallons
(150 L)
OF SALIVA ARE PRODUCED
DAILY IN THE PROCESS.

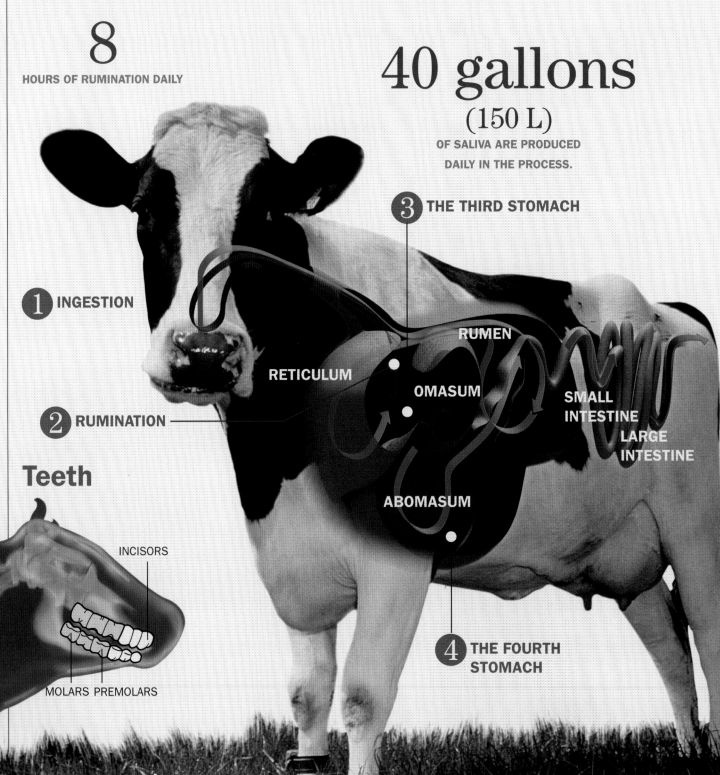

3 THE THIRD STOMACH

1 INGESTION

RUMEN

RETICULUM

OMASUM

SMALL INTESTINE

2 RUMINATION

LARGE INTESTINE

ABOMASUM

Teeth

INCISORS

4 THE FOURTH STOMACH

MOLARS PREMOLARS

DROMEDARY, OR ARABIAN CAMEL
Camelus dromedarius

Habitat	Arabia and Africa
Food	Herbivorous
Average life span	50 years

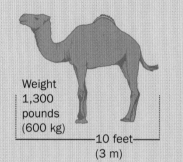

Weight 1,300 pounds (600 kg)

—10 feet— (3 m)

31 pounds (14 kg)

HUMPS CAN WEIGH THIS MUCH.

When water and food are scarce, camels are able to endure by consuming the reserves they have accumulated and stored in the hump and internal sacs.

34 gallons (130 L)

THE AMOUNT OF WATER DROMEDARIES CAN CONSUME IN 10 MINUTES

NOSE

HUMP

HAIR

DROMEDARIES CAN GO WITHOUT FOOD AND WATER FOR

8 days

AT A TEMPERATURE OF 122° F (50° C).

KNEES

Playing Hide and Seek

Just like other species of the animal kingdom, some mammals that live in the wild rely on their bodies' colorations or appearances to disguise their presence. Some mammals imitate objects in their environment, and others take on the appearances of other animals. Zebras' stripes, for example, give these animals a very showy appearance—but when moving in their natural environment, zebras are camouflaged.

Evolutionary Adaptations

Mimicry is defined as the ability of some living beings to imitate the appearance of another living being or an inanimate object in the environment.

STRIPES

SPOTS   OTHER PATTERNS

Different Patterns

In Motion

The patterns of tigers' coats are useful in concealing their outlines, especially when they are moving among the shrubs and bushes of the plains where they hunt.

DISRUPTIVE COLORATION

THE BODY'S CONTOURS ARE BLURRED WHEN SOME SPOTS OF COLOR

ARE MUCH DARKER OR LIGHTER THAN THE REST OF THE COAT.

Part of the Hideaway

PROTECTIVE SURROUNDINGS

Many have a coat that changes color depending on the surroundings.

FUR

Shades and differences of color in the coat are similar to those of tree trunks and dry leaves.

The Great Chain

Maintaining ecological balance requires the existence of prey and predators. Predatorial species bring about a sustained reduction in the number of individuals of the prey species. If predators did not exist, their prey would probably proliferate until the *ecosystem* collapsed, because there would not be enough food for them all.

Equilibrium of the System

Trophic Pyramid

Tertiary Consumers

Secondary Consumers

Primary Consumers

Primary Producers–Plants

Energy Consumed

Population

IS GREATER AS ONE GOES DOWN THE PYRAMID.

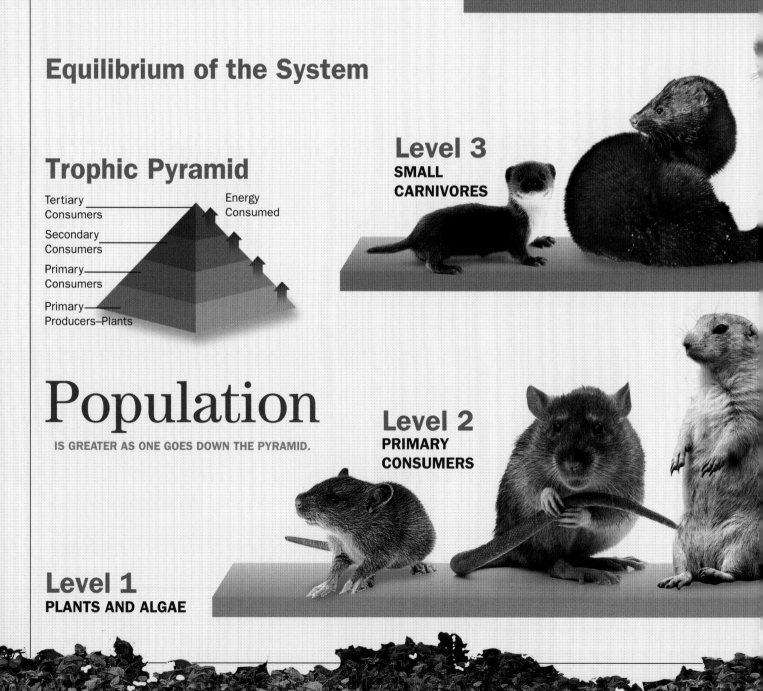

Level 4
LARGE CARNIVORES

SMALL-SPOTTED GENET

Level 3
SMALL CARNIVORES

Level 2
PRIMARY CONSUMERS

Level 1
PLANTS AND ALGAE

WOLF

GEOFFROY'S CAT

SMALL OMNIVORES

Kings of the Jungle

A FOOD CHAIN CAN REACH SEVEN LEVELS.

VARIED DIETS

Scavengers

Eat meat from the animals that are already dead.

Each in Its Place

Nature takes care of maintaining its equilibrium, providing each animal its own role within the food chain. When one of the roles is removed, equilibrium in the region is lost. In Australia, dingoes were a big problem for sheep farmers, who built a great fence to protect their flocks. This barrier left the wild dogs without prey and other species able to move about more freely in search of food. Dingoes are classified as pests both for farm animals as well as for rabies control.

The Introduction of the Dingo

DINGO

KANGAROO
They found greater freedom.

PASTURELANDS
They became scarce.

SHEEP
Their population increased.

DINGO

The Great Fence

was designed to keep dingoes out of the southeastern part of Australia, protecting flocks of sheep. It ran for thousands of miles and was largely successful in its objective.

AUSTRALIA

PERIMETER

SYDNEY

MELBOURNE

ORIGINAL COURSE

CURRENT COURSE | AREA FREE OF DINGOES

3,300 miles
(5,320 km)
THE LENGTH OF THE GREAT FENCE

Kangaroos

4.5 feet
(1.4 m)

5 feet
(1.6 m)

4 feet
(1.3 m)

Family	Macropodidae
Species	*Macropus rufus*

Females are half this size.

Mammals in Society

Social units and mutual aid are common in mammals' lives, except for a few species that live alone or in small families. Here are two examples of mammals with well-defined social structures.

Wolves

VOCAL COMMUNICATION allows wolves to locate pack members.

GAMES

Recognition of Position

High-ranking   Low-ranking

1 ENCOUNTER

2 EXAMINATION

3 RECOGNITION

MARTIAL
EAGLES

Lookout

SIGHT

**MEERKATS ALSO USE
VOCALIZATIONS TO
COMMUNICATE.**

HEAD

VIGILANCE
FROM
ABOVE

Defense

1 SURROUNDING
THE ENEMY

2 ON THEIR BACKS

3 PROTECTION

FRONT PAWS

Meerkats

TRIPOD TAIL

BURROWS

HIND FEET

Territory

Beauty and Height

Finding a female with whom to mate is the great effort of the male's life, a competition with other males of his own species. For stags, antlers play a fundamental role in winning the heart of their chosen one. Whichever stag has the most beautiful, longest, and sharpest horns will be the winner.

ANTLER LAYERS
Epidermis **PERIOSTEUM**
Dermis

Fights

24 inches
(60 cm)

MALE
43 inches
(110 cm)

FEMALE
31 inches
(80 cm)

Red Deer

Order	Artiodactyla
Family	Cervidae
Species	*Cervus elaphus*
Diet	Herbivorous
Weight (male)	400 pounds (180 kg)

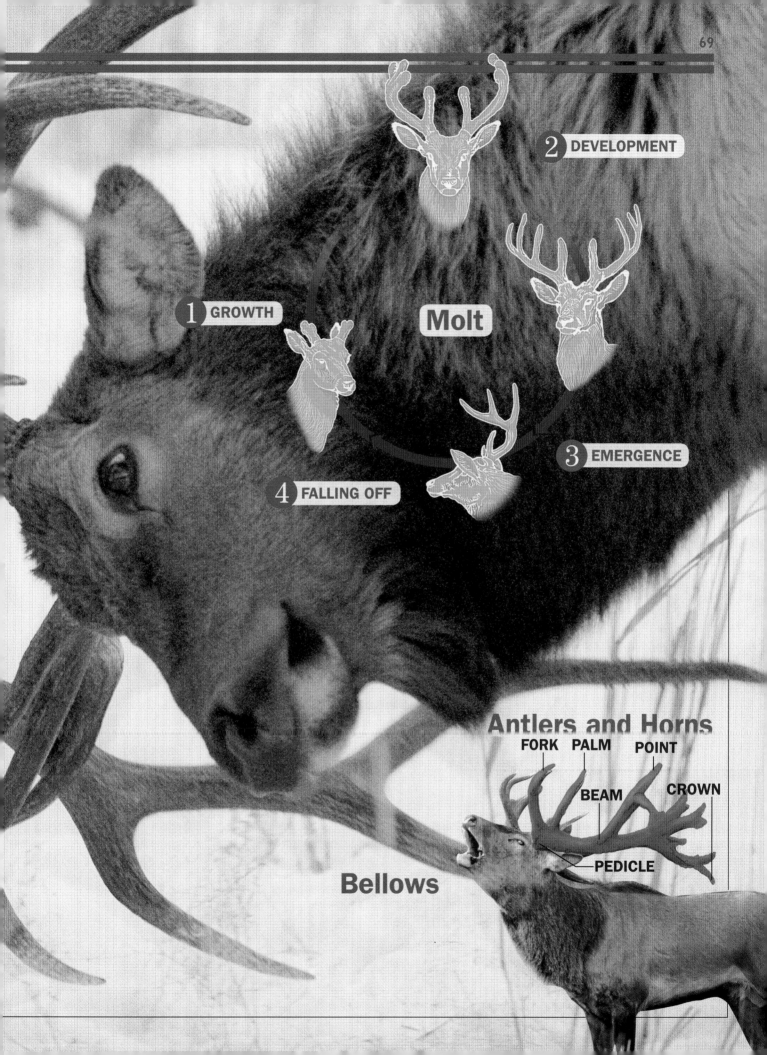

2 DEVELOPMENT

1 GROWTH

Molt

3 EMERGENCE

4 FALLING OFF

Antlers and Horns

FORK PALM POINT

BEAM CROWN

PEDICLE

Bellows

Natural Builders

They have no bricks or cement, but beavers manage to build lodges. They do not work alone, and it is usual for them to act in family groups. Everyone collaborates in building the home, which is generally located next to a river or lake surrounded by forested areas and which can be entered only through aquatic tunnels. Beavers work their whole lives enlarging, repairing, and improving their dwelling.

The Lodge

AMERICAN BEAVER
Castor canadensis

Habitat	Temperate forests in the United States and Canada
Family	Castoridae
Food	Herbivorous

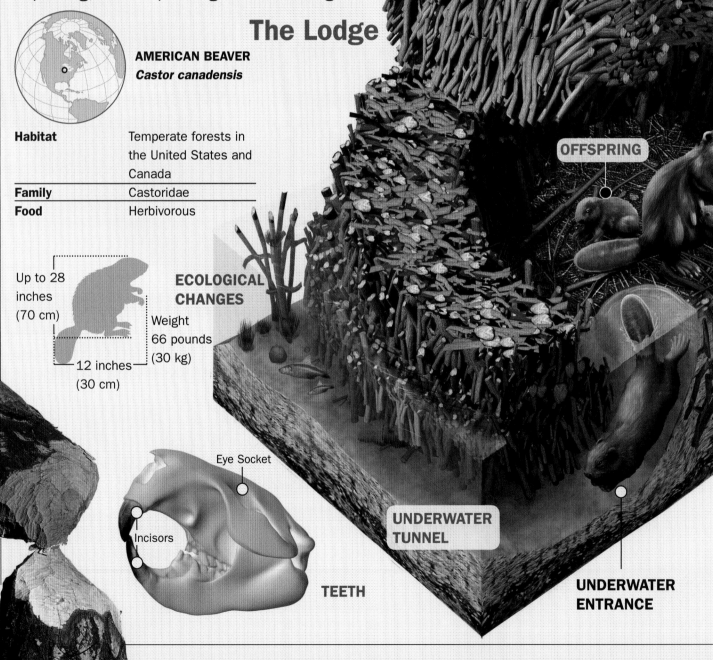

Up to 28 inches (70 cm)

12 inches (30 cm)

Weight 66 pounds (30 kg)

ECOLOGICAL CHANGES

Eye Socket

Incisors

TEETH

OFFSPRING

UNDERWATER TUNNEL

UNDERWATER ENTRANCE

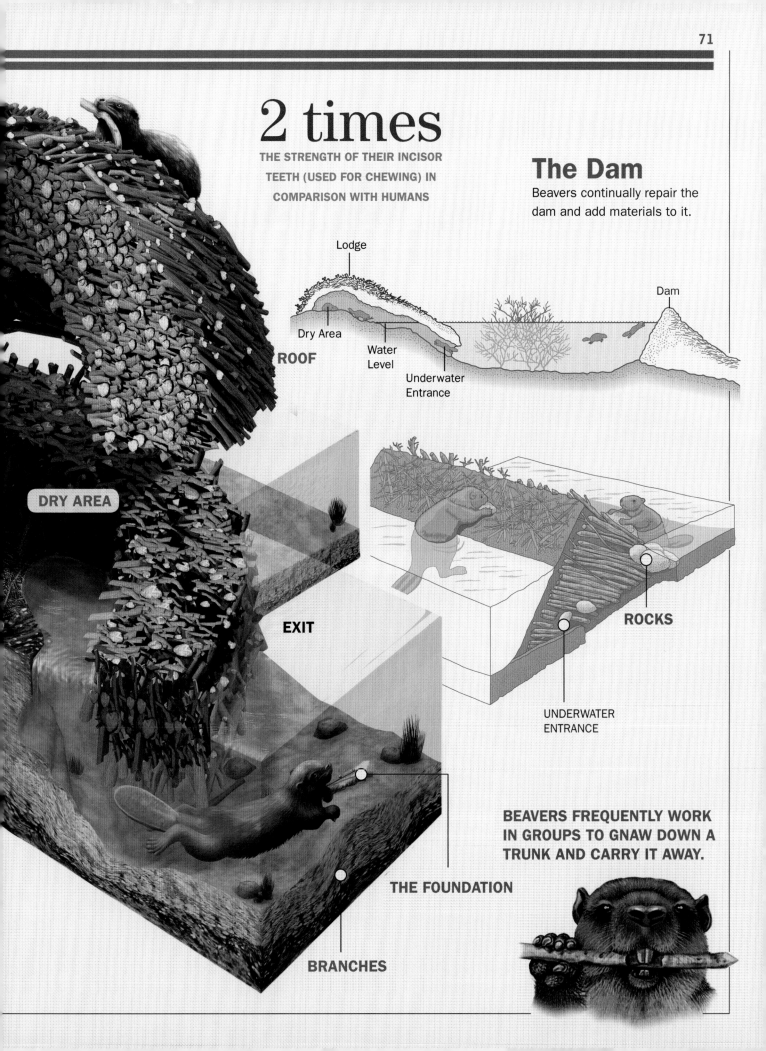

2 times

THE STRENGTH OF THEIR INCISOR TEETH (USED FOR CHEWING) IN COMPARISON WITH HUMANS

The Dam

Beavers continually repair the dam and add materials to it.

Lodge

Dry Area

ROOF

Water Level

Underwater Entrance

Dam

DRY AREA

EXIT

ROCKS

UNDERWATER ENTRANCE

BEAVERS FREQUENTLY WORK IN GROUPS TO GNAW DOWN A TRUNK AND CARRY IT AWAY.

THE FOUNDATION

BRANCHES

Lively Tunnels

Rabbits are social animals that live in colonies in a series of burrows called warrens. The burrows are dug underground and are inhabited by females of high social rank. Rabbits are principally *nocturnal* and spend most of the day hidden in the burrow, leaving to eat when night falls.

PREFERRED PLACES

200 feet (60 m)
IS THE FARTHEST A RABBIT WILL WILLINGLY GO FROM ITS BURROW

ENTRANCE TO THE WARREN 6 inches (15 cm)

Hind Foot

DANGER SIGNAL

SONIC ALERT

Warren

FOOD DEPOSIT

NEST

PROTECTED INTERIOR

1 FRONT FEET

2 HIND FEET

3 NEW HOP

RABBIT FOOTPRINT PATTERNS

SECONDARY
ENTRANCE

Secondary Corridors

are often not interconnected.

DIET
They feed on grassy plants, roots, and bulbs.

5 to 8 inches
(12-20 cm)
FOOD CELLARS

3 to 10 feet
(1-3 m)
LIVING AREAS

130 feet (40 m)
IS HOW LONG A BURROW TUNNEL CAN BE.

What Doesn't Run, Flies

They are meteors of flesh, bone, and hot blood. Cheetahs are the fastest of the land animals. They can reach over 70 miles per hour (115 km/h) in short runs. However, they can sustain a speed over 60 miles (100 km/hr) for only a few seconds.

TAKEOFF

Cheetahs

1 START

2 SPINAL CONTRACTION

NOSTRILS

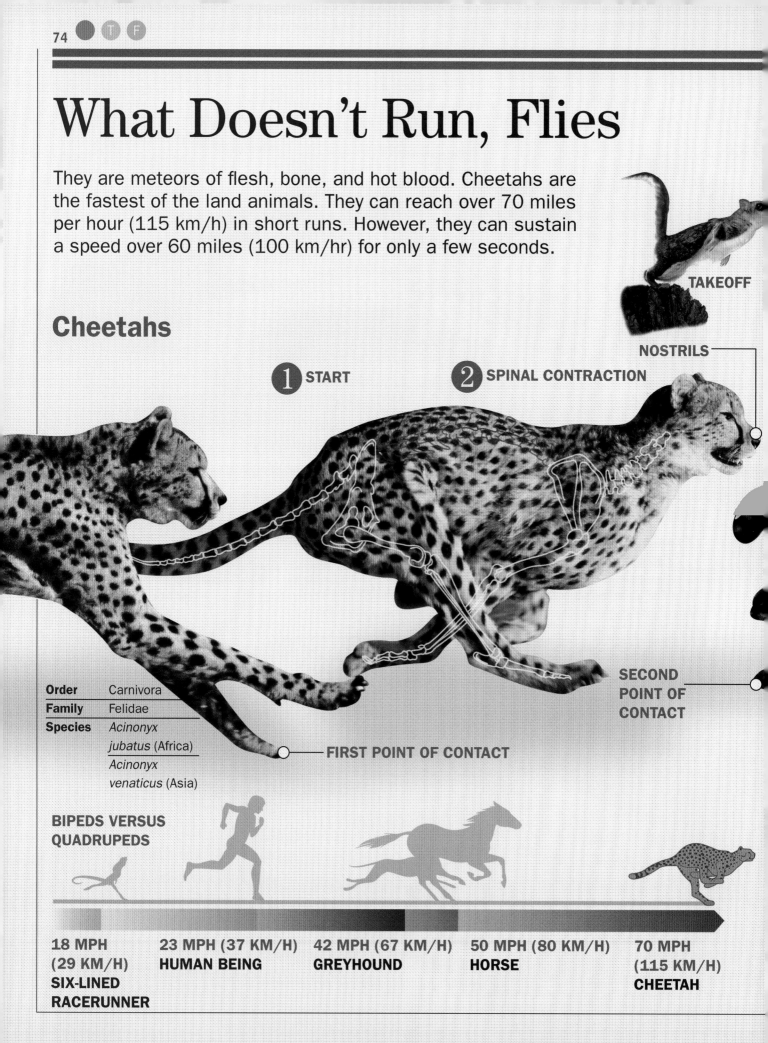

SECOND POINT OF CONTACT

FIRST POINT OF CONTACT

Order	Carnivora
Family	Felidae
Species	*Acinonyx jubatus* (Africa)
	Acinonyx venaticus (Asia)

BIPEDS VERSUS QUADRUPEDS

18 MPH (29 KM/H) SIX-LINED RACERUNNER	23 MPH (37 KM/H) HUMAN BEING	42 MPH (67 KM/H) GREYHOUND	50 MPH (80 KM/H) HORSE	70 MPH (115 KM/H) CHEETAH

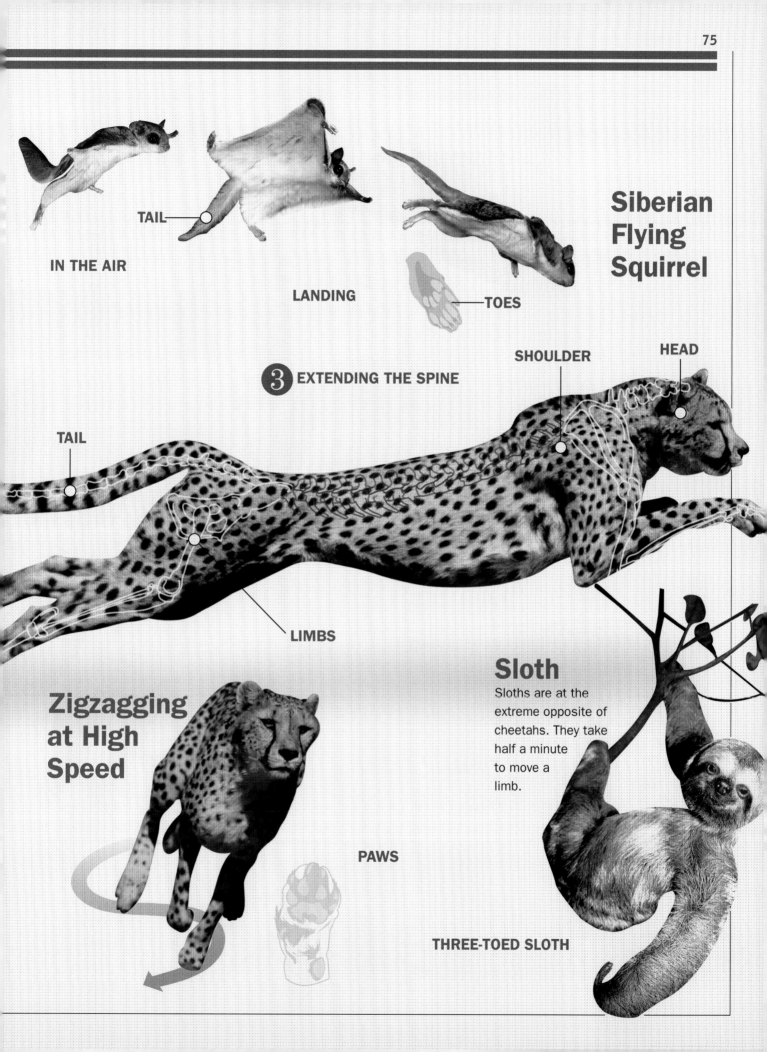

TAIL

IN THE AIR

LANDING

TOES

Siberian Flying Squirrel

3 EXTENDING THE SPINE

SHOULDER

HEAD

TAIL

LIMBS

Zigzagging at High Speed

PAWS

Sloth

Sloths are at the extreme opposite of cheetahs. They take half a minute to move a limb.

THREE-TOED SLOTH

Speed Records

Most birds fly between 25 and 40 miles per hour (40 and 70 km/h), but the fastest birds can beat the cheetah for speed. Other birds amaze us with their endurance, the altitude they can reach, and their ability to travel over long distances. See how birds and other animals compare below.

Air

DRAGONFLY
The fastest flying insect

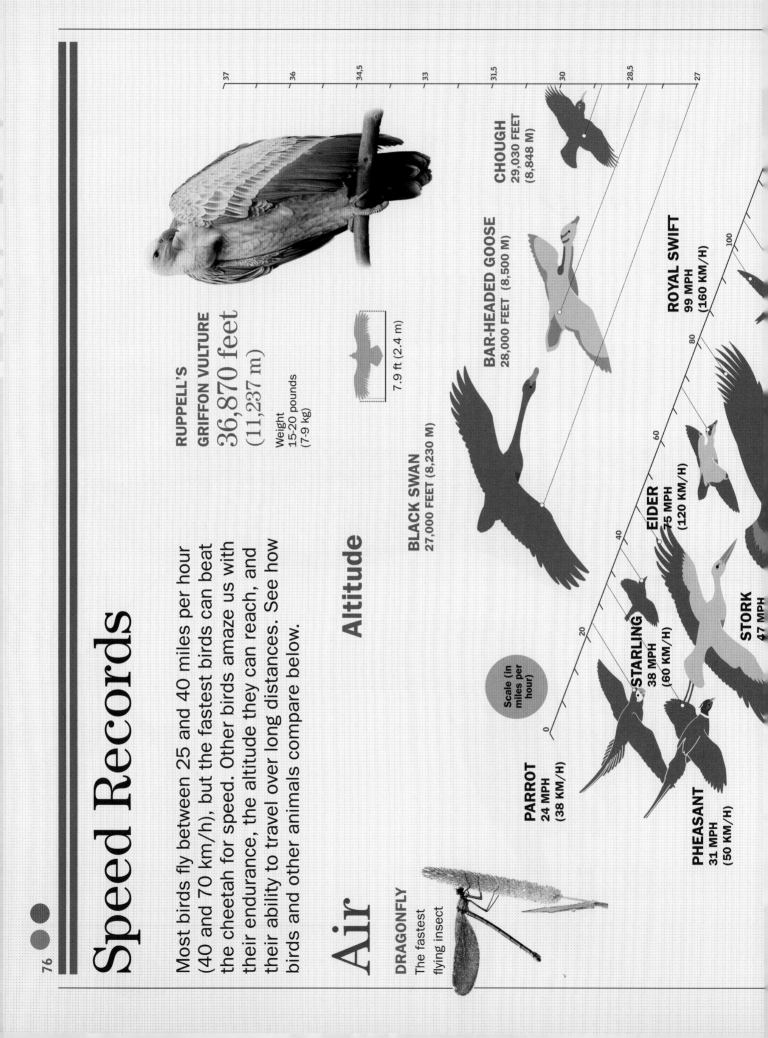

RUPPELL'S GRIFFON VULTURE
36,870 feet
(11,237 m)

Weight
15-20 pounds
(7-9 kg)

7.9 ft (2.4 m)

Altitude

BLACK SWAN
27,000 FEET (8,230 M)

BAR-HEADED GOOSE
28,000 FEET (8,500 M)

CHOUGH
29,030 FEET
(8,848 M)

Scale (in miles per hour)

0   20   40   60   80   100

PARROT
24 MPH
(38 KM/H)

PHEASANT
31 MPH
(50 KM/H)

STARLING
38 MPH
(60 KM/H)

STORK
47 MPH

EIDER
75 MPH
(120 KM/H)

ROYAL SWIFT
99 MPH
(160 KM/H)

37   36   34.5   33   31.5   30   28.5   27

Land

ELEPHANT
17 MPH (28 KM/H)

HARE
20 MPH
(32 KM/H)

GIRAFFE
30 MPH
(50 KM/H)

ROYAL EAGLE
81 MPH
(130 KM/H)

SPINE TAILED SWIFT
106 MPH (171 KM/H)

OSTRICH
45 MPH
(72 KM/H)

PRONGHORN
55 MPH (88 KM/H)

CHEETAH
65 mph
(105 km/h)

PEREGRINE FALCON
200 mph
(320 km/h)

32–45 in
(80–115 cm)

18–20 in
(45–50 cm)

Scale
(in miles
per hour)
Land-Water

0   10   20   30   40   50   60   70   80   90   100

Water

DOLPHIN
22 MPH
(35 KM/H)

GENTOO PENGUIN
22.4 MPH (36 KM/H)

SEI WHALE
30 MPH
(48 KM/H)

SAILFISH
50 MPH
(80 KM/H)

TUNA
62 mph
(100 km/h)

20   29   38   47   56   65

Distance and Endurance

ARCTIC TERN

**RUFOUS
HUMMINGBIRD**

GOLDEN PLOVER

Weight
0.1–0.2 ounce
(4–6 g)

4 in
(10 cm)

Nocturnal Flight

Bats are the only mammals that can fly. Their forelimbs have been transformed into hands with very long fingers joined together by a membrane (called the patagium) that forms the surface of the wing.

Expert Pilots

Their Radar

1 The signal strikes the object around it.

2 The signal bounces back.

60 miles per hour

(97 km)

THE SPEED SOME BATS MAY REACH DURING FLIGHT

THUMB

HUMERUS **RADIUS**

SECOND FINGER

FOURTH FINGER

THIRD FINGER

PATAGIUM

Hibernation

These bats spend the winter in a lethargic state hanging by their feet, faces down, in caves and other dark places.

FRUIT BAT (Franquet's Epauletted Bat)
Epomops franqueti

Habitat	Forests of Ghana and Congo
Family	Pteropodae
Length of wingspan	14 inches (36 cm)

1

2

3

4

5

HAND OR WING

ELASTIC FIBERS

Flexible Wings

UROPATAGIUM

The Human Threat

Over the next 30 years, almost a quarter of the mammals could disappear from the face of the Earth, according to the United Nations. Experts calculate that more than 1,000 mammals are endangered or vulnerable.

Orangutan

KEY
- MAMMALS AT CRITICAL RISK
- ○ UP TO 10 SPECIES ALREADY EXTINCT
- ● MORE THAN 10 SPECIES ALREADY EXTINCT

Sea Otter

MORE THAN ONE OUT OF EVERY

5

SPECIES OF MAMMALS IS ENDANGERED.

HAINAN BLACK-CRESTED GIBBON

DAMA GAZELLE

HIPPOPOTAMUS

CHINCHILLA

SOUTHERN RIGHT WHALE

CETACEANS

Dolphin   Harbor Porpoise

Sperm Whale   Blue Whale

Gray Whale   Fin Whale

Giant Panda